P9-BIB-214

Stockton

"Stockton's Enterprises" by
Stephen Ferris

Produced in cooperation with the
City of Stockton Office of Economic Development

Windsor Publications, Inc.
Chatsworth, California

Stockton

Heart of the Valley

A Contemporary Portrait By Charles Clerc

Windsor Publications, Inc.—Book Division
Managing Editor: Karen Story
Design Director: Alexander d'Anca
Photo Director: Susan L. Wells
Executive Editor: Pamela Schroeder

Staff for *Stockton: Heart of the Valley*
Manuscript Editors: Amy Adelstein, Jerry Mosher
Photo Editors: Cameron Cox, William Matthews
Senior Editor, Corporate Profiles: Judith L. Hunter
Production Editor, Corporate Profiles: Albert Polito
Customer Service Manager: Phyllis Feldman-Schroeder
Proofreader: Liz Reuben
Editorial Assistants: Kim Kievman, Michael Nugwynne, Michele Oakley, Kathy B. Peyser, Susan Schlanger, Theresa J. Solis
Publisher's Representatives, Corporate Profiles: Paul Williams, Gina Woolf, Harriet Holmes
Designer: Christina L. Rosepapa
Layout Artist, Corporate Profiles: Bonnie Felt
Layout Artist, Editorial: Michael Burg

Library of Congress Cataloging-in-Publication Data
Clerc, Charles. Stockton, heart of the valley : a contemporary portrait / by Charles Clerc —1st ed.
p. 176 cm. 23x31
Bibliography: p. 171
Includes index
ISBN 0-89781-324-3
1. Stockton (Calif.)—History. 2. Stockton (Calif.)—Description—Views. 3. Stockton (Calif.)—Industries. I. Title.
F869.S8C57 1989 89-8944 979.4′55—dc20
CIP

Published 1989
Printed in the United States of America
First Edition

Windsor Publications, Inc.
Elliot Martin, Chairman of the Board
James L. Fish III, Chief Operating Officer
Michele Sylvestro, Vice President, Sales/Marketing

FRONTISPIECE: The rich delta waters around Stockton sustain an abundance of crops. Photo by Mark E. Gibson

FACING PAGE: The Stockton Memorial Civic Auditorium is seen here through the cascading waters of Fremont Park's fountain. Photo by Mark E. Gibson

STOCKTON
CIVIC

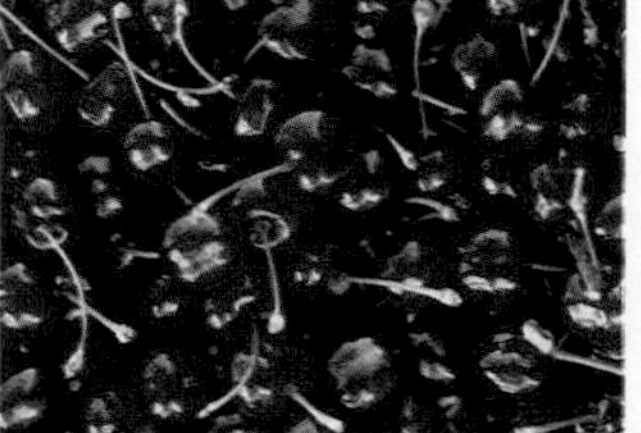

Contents

Acknowledgments

I am grateful for the helpful commentary of the following people who read part of this book in manuscript form: Olive Davis, Patricia Sangster-Franklin, Arlen J. Hansen, Raymond W. Hillman, George Lewis, Audree O'Connell, Dianne Runion, Jim Shebl, David Smith, William N. Sousa, and Joe Travale.

Many thanks to them, and a special thank you to Mary Weil for her technical help.

A brilliant orange sunset highlights the downtown corridor and its surrounding waterways. Photo by Kerrick James

Part **1**

Dynamic City on the Delta

A world of rich blue sky and fertile soil, the land around Stockton basks in temperate weather, pleasing living conditions, and a sunny economic outlook. Photo by Steve Pereira

Chapter **1**

The Good Life

Originally named after a naval commodore back in the mid-nineteenth century, Stockton is multifaceted enough to have earned a variety of epithets since: California's Sunrise Seaport, California's Crossroads, Harbor of the Heartlands, Gateway to the Delta, California's Cornucopia, City for All Seasons, not to mention Brick City and Tree City and Fat City. More of these labels will come and go, but Stockton will always be recognized as the Heart of the Valley that links Sea and Sierra.

The epithets all point to a fine place where the quality of life is high. Simultaneously brisk and relaxed, vibrant and laid back, Stockton is a city whose convenient location, mild weather, moderate size, flourishing commerce, and ethnic diversity

The architecture of the Bank of Stockton building exemplifies Stockton's low-key urban image. Photo by Kerrick James

make it an ideal place to live.

Stockton crowns a long, wide valley between the Pacific Ocean and the Mother Lode leading to the high Sierra. Flat as a pool table, laced with waterways, it sits amid farmlands considered among the richest and most productive in the world. Notably Stockton is an inland port, 75 nautical miles east of the Golden Gate, joined to the Pacific by a channel large enough for most ocean-going vessels.

Many a city around the country would sell its soul for Stockton's location: the Bay Area along one side, the Sierra along the other; San Francisco to the west, Lake Tahoe to the northeast, Yosemite to the southeast, the state capital to the north, all within easy driving distance. Yet it's no mere way station amid all these attractions; Stockton is home to nearly 200,000 people, making it the 13th-largest city in California. And Stockton and its immediate environs (not including, of course, Sacramento to the north or Modesto to the south) number about 300,000 residents.

Think about looking at a blue vault of sky for weeks on end. It gives you surefire conversational openers. Like: "Do you remember that time we didn't see a cloud for four months?" "Well, whadya expect when the sun shines an average of 240 days a year!" "Did you ever see a sunset so beautiful?—peach and mauve and lavender and rose and gold." "Yup, we could use some rain."

Zealous Stocktonians will concede that occasionally the heat of July and August and even September gets a bit out of hand, as does the occasional fog of late fall, December, and January. These momentary lapses of weather are meant to keep them from crowing about constant temperateness. After all, they'll say, no place is absolutely perfect.

Then they haul out their statistics, and the crowing starts all over again: an average temperature of 74 degrees, 52 days of rain a year, an average annual rainfall of 14 inches, three thunderstorms a year, 26 percent average humidity, and winters during which the thermometer plunges all the way to the 40s and the 30s. That's of course above zero.

And they remind you that it never snows (well, except for that one time back in 1916) and the breezes are gentle (well, most of the time). Admittedly, a stranger coming from, say, the Rocky Mountains, the Midwest, or the East might miss the sharp demarcations of the seasons. But not for long. It isn't difficult to get used

Like trees at an oasis, office buildings cluster around the nourishing flow of the harbor's commercial activity. The city is a distribution center for farm products leaving from surrounding land and incoming commodities bound for Sacramento and the rest of the country. Photo by Kerrick James

to good weather. The key to customer satisfaction is cool evenings. Temperatures may soar during the day, but every night—guaranteed—is comfortable for sleeping.

In sum, Stockton weather stays milder than most places throughout the world. You have the word of its natives, pale or sunbronzed. (Qualification to become a native takes 90 days, give or take a few for good behavior.)

Stockton's moderate size has advantages too: big enough to provide most services, but not yet suffering from the consequences of uncontrolled growth. The city conveys spaciousness and openness—here you can swell your chest and breathe deeply. There's no urban blight to speak of, and traffic remains manageable though here and there it is starting to get snarly.

The city prides itself on keeping a low profile, literally. The tallest buildings are in the 9- to 12-story range. And Stockton doesn't go for showy outdoor advertising. Despite some obvious exceptions, downtown and north of the Calaveras, it tries to enforce an ordinance against signs of excessive size or garish neon. Stockton isn't exactly Carmel, but it deliberately eschews the flash and glitter of some gaudier California and Nevada cities. It's a city easy on the eye, a small town in a big-town body. Make that a big town in a small-town body.

The dollar stretches in Stockton. Here's a place where people can afford to live. By comparison with the Bay Area, land values are low, prices are reasonable, and housing has remained relatively affordable. These facts have contributed to the popularity of Stockton, particularly for many commuters who work in San Francisco and Oakland.

Of course, this commuting has intensified freeway travel. But if traffic is

RIGHT: On a clear night by the waterfront, lights and shadows paint the water and walkways of the city's North Park. Photo by Mark E. Gibson

FACING PAGE, TOP: Stockton is a magnet for young families, with its affordable housing and commuter access to Bay Area cities. Photo by Kerrick James

unpleasant at times in Stockton and vicinity, it's never horrendous, as it can easily get an hour or two away in the Bay Area.

Any contemplation of Stockton and the Delta will bring to mind images of boats. Boats and sparkling water. Motorboats, sailboats, houseboats, yachts, cargo vessels, tankers, all moving in and around a city blessed with waterways. Boats are everywhere—in the channels, the rivers, the inlets and coves, the sloughs that extend like capillaries into a thousand miles of waterways in three directions from Stockton.

A familiar image: a 27-foot sailboat tacking in the channel, the wind puffing its sails in the setting sun; another, a water skier slapping along behind the veed trough of a speedboat. The eye then fixes on a bend of land, and suddenly looming over the banks of the levees is a huge cargo vessel coming into Stockton through its inland Deep Water Channel to pick up a load of cotton for Taiwan, coal or beet pulp pellets for Japan, almonds for the Soviet Union, sulfur for India, dried milk for Brazil, calcined clay for Rotterdam, copper for Germany and Korea. Or the ships come in low, down to their Plimsoll marks, laden with steel or anhydrous ammonia or cement or other cargo, to be transported by truck or rail to all parts of the United States. A series of final images occur at Christmastime: a procession of boats along the channel to the downtown marina, the channel lined with thousands of spectators entranced by the Christmas decorations and Christmas lights bedecking boats of all sizes and shapes, a parade of Santas and angels and stars, twinkling reds and silvers and greens and blues and golds.

The many navigable waterways around Stockton, including two main rivers, the San Joaquin and the farther Sacramento, bespeak accessibility in all other ways. Two major north-south highway systems—Interstate 5 and Highway 99—connect at Stockton and link not far off to 80 east and west and to 580 west. The new crosstown freeway, nearing completion through the heart of the inner city, serves as a convenient locus for Highways 99 and 5. Moreover, Stockton is served twice daily by Amtrak and round-the-clock by Greyhound bus lines. Moderate sized but growing Metropolitan Airport, located a few miles south of the city, is presently served by USAir and United Express Airlines. While Stocktonians may wish for more stability in the local airline business and for more flights to specific locations, such as the Bay Area, service is otherwise considered adequate, especially to Los Angeles. Once serving as gateway to the mines of the Mother Lode and long since recognized as a natural crossroads, Stockton has become a transportation hub for the entire state.

The people of Stockton are as ethnically diverse as its ways of life. The city contains a large population of European stock, of black and Hispanic, of Filipino and Japanese and Chinese, and an increasing number of new immigrants from Southeast Asia, such as Vietnamese, Cambodians, Thais, and Laotians, including a large Hmong community. Within the same few square miles you'll find a Buddhist temple, a Jewish synagogue, a Greek basilica, a Latter-Day Saints ward, and a Methodist church. A gauge of the city's ethnic diversity is its more than 500 restaurants. Dozens of these specialize in cuisine that is Mexican, French, Basque, Filipino, Italian, Chinese, Greek, Japanese, German, and Vietnamese. In addition, these various groups celebrate their national origins in colorful

***BELOW:* Pleasure craft of all description ply the diverse waterways that stretch in all directions from the city. Photo by Steve Pereira**

national festivals.

Unlike many cities that divide into topographically diverse parts and distinctly named neighborhoods, Stockton's areas tend to meld into one another, although geographical distinctions can be made, such as Central Stockton, Southeast Stockton, and North Stockton.

The designation "north" has different meanings. Like so many cities, Stockton's growth has been toward the north and outward in successive stages, from long-established neighborhoods to recent, to new, to brand-new developments; from the Calaveras River to Benjamin Holt, to Hammer Lane, and now increasingly north from Hammer to Eight Mile Road. To a lesser extent, similar developments are spreading outward in the south.

Just add water—Sacramento Valley soil and sunshine are among the best in the world for agriculture. Photo by John Elk III

The growth is taking place along freeways and out into previously productive farmland. Thus, land that once sprouted crops now sprouts houses.

Nevertheless, the surrounding land remains as rich as ever. It's probably not true that if you took a bare stick and shoved it into the soil it would grow tall. But it certainly would begin to sprout and show a few leaves. (Stocktonians boast about the fecundity of their land too.) And why not—the land in San Joaquin County surrounding Stockton is ranked, on the average, seventh richest in the United States in terms of productivity, to the tune of three-quarters of a billion dollars annually.

Eighty farm products come from this soil, to make a mighty contribution to the world's food basket: vegetables of every kind, including tomatoes (the biggest revenue-producing crop), beans, onions, corn, sugar beets, cucumbers, asparagus (the most popular vegetable and second in gross value); all kinds of grains; fruits and nuts, including cherries, walnuts, almonds, apricots, peaches, and, most significantly, grapes—ranked among the world's finest—that contribute to California's fine wines. Milk, eggs, and cattle and calves bring in well over $200 million annually.

The Delta area alone contains a third of a million acres on crop-producing islands amid the waterways. A drive along backroads reveals California's cornucopia: field upon field, orchard upon orchard, vineyard upon vineyard. That verdancy is evident everywhere you look around Stockton: its thriving lawns and flower gardens and the 150,000 trees that line its streets and shade its

A great American institution begins here in these truckloads of ripe tomatoes—catsup. Spaghetti sauce is another specialty of the region's food processing industry. Photo by John Elk III

numerous parks. The trees range from majestic valley oaks to elm and ash and poplar to giant palms. These and others are city maintained. If you count the trees that fill residential lots, you could multiply by five and thus deduce the city's moniker, Tree City.

As those trees depend upon their roots, Stockton depends upon the lifeblood of its commerce. Indeed, the action of the human heart can be likened to the workings of an economic system. The analogue holds for Stockton as the heart of the valley in the way it circulates goods, commodities, and services. Neither mill town nor mining community, neither silicon valley nor aerospace center, Stockton relies upon diversification. No single industry dominates the city.

The sights and sounds of business enterprise are everywhere. Stockton is home to small manufacturing plants, to distribution centers, to canneries and processors and other forms of agribusiness, to home and building construction, to thriftily automated production, to transportation, and to a variety of banks and retail trades and other services. One of the nation's largest savings banks is headquartered in Stockton. Health care services have grown with the expansion of four large hospitals, and more seem to be coming. In terms of recent annual income, the Port of Stockton ranks second to Oakland and well ahead of San Francisco, Sacramento, and Richmond. Significantly, new businesses are moving in all the time.

Students from 40 states and 60 countries attend the University of the Pacific (UOP), California's oldest chartered university (1851). A university with the reputation and look of an Ivy League school, it enrolls close to 4,000 students at its Stockton campus. Its McGeorge School of Law in Sacramento enrolls more than a thousand, and half that number train in its dental school in San Francisco, for a total enrollment of 5,500. Students traditionally complain about college towns not meeting their needs, and UOP is no exception. But this irony is worth noting: nearly a fourth of UOP students who attend the central campus from elsewhere wind up after graduation settling in Stockton and its environs.

Also nearby is an excellent community college in San Joaquin Delta College, with a student body of some 15,000. And small private colleges, like Humphreys, are available too.

Recreation, sports, and cultural attractions abound. A montage begins with a toddler giggling as she pets a rabbit in the shade of a tuneful merry-go-round at Pixie Woods, a children's play park. A music lover settles back into a deep red

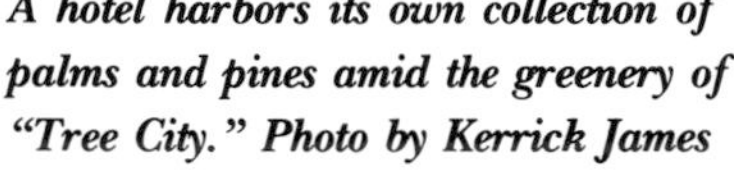

A hotel harbors its own collection of palms and pines amid the greenery of "Tree City." Photo by Kerrick James

Students from around the world come to study at Stockton's universities and colleges. Many of them fall in love with the area and never leave. Photo by Steve Pereira

plush chair as the strains of Beethoven from the 50-year-old Stockton Symphony Orchestra loft through Atherton Auditorium. A full-throated roar comes up from a packed crowd of 6,000 at the university's Spanos Center, where the twice national-champion women's volleyball team rallies to take match point. A lone fisherman stands on a bank at Dad's Point, patiently awaiting that bite from a giant sturgeon, striped bass, or catfish; so what if this time he snags some weeds? A film crew up from Hollywood lines a Stockton street with its vans and trucks and elaborate cabling as it prepares a scene from one of the many movies shot in this area. During a blustery day a youthful windsurfer skims past a couple in a paddle-boat on one of the many man-made lakes centered in housing developments throughout the city's varied northern sites. A quadrant of softball fields at Louis Park is alive with light and color and motion on a balmy summer night as eight of Stockton's 453 softball teams compete in women's and men's leagues. Off in the marshy Delta, thousands of migrating birds—ducks, geese, curlews, cranes—take to the skies or settle in for a brief respite.

All of these images come together in Stockton, the good place, where agriculture, industry, culture, education, services, and leisure activities all mesh to create an appealing life-style in an enterprising, dynamic community. Yes, on occasion our thermometers wince over a stretch of sizzling summer days; yes, we have our pockets of poverty; yes, unemployment presents problems, especially in the winter season; yes, like most cities, our crime figures need to be lower; yes, from time to time some of our citizens aren't too happy with our city government; but most—truly most—would concur that Stockton is an excellent place to live.

At the peak of the 1920s, when the city economy was thriving, members of the Chamber of Commerce took an excursion on the J.D. Peters *in recognition of the successful delta farms along the 1,000-mile-long waterway. Courtesy, Stockton Chamber of Commerce*

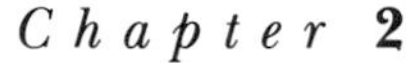

Chapter 2

Yesterday to Today

Before the Stockton of today, before the Fat City of the 1950s and the Tuleburg of the 1840s, before the Indian villages of the 1700s, much of the region resembled a huge fen: an intermingling of marshes and sloughs, tules, and mosses. It contained a third of a million acres of peat land. Peat is decomposed plant matter—in other words, an organic compost. This deep peat came to produce amazingly rich farmland. But many years were to pass before levees were built, islands created, and the land planted with bounteous crops. Farther inland, all the way into the foothills, lay thousands of acres of prime land, forested by oaks and willows and brush. The Stockton area itself east of the waterways consisted of flat grassland and thriving groves of valley oak.

Charles M. Weber, a German immigrant who traveled to America when he was 22, went on to become the founder of Stockton. Courtesy, Stockton Public Library

Indians of various groups—Yokuts in the central valley, Maidu to the northeast and, beyond them, Mintum, and in the central delta, Miwok and Mokelkos—hunted and fished and bartered, and occasionally fought. The great valley teamed with life: waterfowl and birds, salmon, bass, catfish, beaver, gopher, squirrel, muskrat, deer, antelope, grizzly bear, and tule elk. In the location of what was to become Stockton, Indians sailed their tule balsas from place to place. When the waters rose, this area became a floodplain.

Sadly, the Indians were to die off in great numbers from remittent fever, or specifically malaria and smallpox, their population plummeting from an estimated high of 30,000 to less than 1,000. The incursions of the white man and his diseases certainly contributed to the demise of native Americans.

At times from afar the Delta waterways looked like a sea of glass. The first Europeans to view them, in March 1772 as they stood on the slopes of Mount Diablo, were the Spanish: Pedro Fages; Father Juan Crespi, who was a chaplain and diarist; and a small band of soldiers. No wonder they thought they had discovered an inland sea.

Over the next decades the Spanish explored the Delta farther and farther upstream. Later came trapper-explorers like Jedediah Smith and French-Canadian trappers of the Hudson's Bay Company, plying their trade for furs, especially beaver.

Often hostilities erupted between the Indians and the Spanish, but in the Mexican era after 1821 friendly relations were established with the Indians by Michel La Framboise, a Hudson's Bay trapper, who worked out of a seasonal bivouac of what was later to become French Camp.

In 1844 Captain John C. Frémont and his guide Kit Carson headed south through the San Joaquin Valley, camping overnight along a site approximately where Waterloo Road is today. The first building in Stockton was a tule hut built by Thomas Lindsey in 1844 on the site of what is now Stockton City Hall. The following spring Lindsey died in an attack by Indians.

Development of most places begins with the vision of one individual. Charles M. Weber is that person for Stockton. Like John Sutter in Sacramento or Alonzo Horton in San Diego, Weber saw potentialities beneath the rawness.

Born in Steinwenden in the Homburg area of West Germany, son of a minister, Weber dreamed of going to America and finally set sail in 1836 at the age of

22. His meteoric rise would set him apart from millions of other enterprising immigrants because in hardly more than a decade he would found a city and strike it rich.

Naval officer Robert F. Stockton, who helped Charles M. Weber recuperate from his time spent in captivity, was rewarded for his efforts when Weber named his new town after him. Courtesy, Stockton Chamber of Commerce

When he first arrived in the U.S., Weber spent time in New Orleans and St. Louis; in 1841 he headed to California with the Bidwell-Bartleson party, a band of 32 men, a woman, and a child. Once in California, Weber visited Sutter, a German-speaking Swiss, at New Helvetia (an early name for Sacramento). Sutter employed him for a year as an overseer. Next Weber worked as a merchant for two years in San Jose. There he met Guillermo (William) Gulnac, a 41-year-old native New Yorker and blacksmith, who was to become his business partner.

Gulnac had been given a huge land grant by Mexican governor Manuel Micheltorena to El Rancho del Campo de Los Franceses (French Camp Ranch), an area encompassing 11 square leagues, or 48,747 acres. In April 1845, thinking it was too late to prove the grant, Gulnac sold this huge tract to Weber for 179 pesos (100 pesos in silver and 79 pesos in merchandise). This deal of the century can be compared, on a much smaller scale of course, with an earlier purchase of a certain New York island for pocket change and trinkets.

At this time, when he was still a San Jose businessman, Weber had already adopted his "California" name Carlos Maria Weber (his given name was Karl David), and he was soon to become known as Captain Weber. The rank of captain was first bestowed upon him by Mexican General José Castro at the outbreak of hostilities between rival Mexican factions in California. Weber and a party of volunteers had kept Micheltorena from taking over San Jose.

The precipitating event in this conflict occurred when American rebels, chafing against Mexican rule, raised a bear flag over Sonoma on June 14, 1846. Weber contributed to the revolt by conscripting horses—and, due to his methods, alienating friends—though he never did any actual fighting. Later on Weber was made a captain of cavalry by John B. Montgomery, a naval captain. History books continue to refer to him as Captain Weber.

For refusing to fight against the Bear Flag rebels and for secretly raising a defense force, Weber was taken prisoner and held captive by the Mexican government. General Castro, a Californio, understood Weber's position but could hardly approve it. While retreating south, Castro took Weber, along with other prisoners, into the Southern California desert. Near the Colorado River Castro re-

During the California Gold Rush, Stockton served as a supply center for the southernmost mines, and tents, huts, and simple wood-frame stores seemed to spring up everywhere. This lithograph of a W.H. Creasey painting commissioned by Charles M. Weber depicts the frontier town of Stockton in 1849. Courtesy, Stockton Chamber of Commerce

leased Weber, who made it alone back to Los Angeles.

There Weber met Commodore Robert Field Stockton, who was securing Los Angeles against the Mexicans. Stockton had been in charge of Monterey, the Mexican capital of California, and served as commander of American forces in California in July 1846. The two men got along well. Stockton helped Weber to recuperate; he also promised to help Weber develop his new town by increasing shipping in the channel, particularly by furnishing a schooner for passenger-supply service, and to help confirm Weber's huge land grant.

Shortly thereafter Weber would express his thanks by naming the town he founded after the naval officer, the first community in California not to have a Spanish or an Indian name. The problem is that Stockton never kept his word. The story goes that in time Weber, put off by the commodore's unfulfilled promises, preferred the name of his summer home site, Castoria, for the town, but Stockton it remained. Perish the thought: we could have been called Castoroilians, rather than Stocktonians.

Weber moved to his undeveloped rancho on the San Joaquin River in 1847. Three years before, he had become a Mexican citizen to be eligible to own land. (Purportedly, too, the Protestant Weber then had to convert to Catholicism, though other evidence shows he converted at a later date to marry a Catholic.) His budding town grew around a body of water named McLeod Lake, after Alex McLeod, a veteran trapper of the 1820s. The lake was well situated at the head of the main channel amidst the confluence of five sloughs.

Weber was good at making friends with Indians, and settlement succeeded in part because of his amicable relations with Si-yak-umna Indian chief José Jesus (1799-1855). Peace proved advantageous to both sides. José Jesus, who had been hostile toward Mexican authorities, assured the safety of his own people by his handshake with Weber.

Then occurred the event that would alter Weber's tiny village forever: the discovery of gold at Sutter's Mill in Coloma in 1848. Thousands of get-rich-quickers poured into the region. A flourishing tent city sprang up, within 50 miles of gold country. Alongside the tents of canvas and calico, huts of willow and tule were thrown together. Rough plank boxes became simple frame stores.

As supply center for the southernmost mines, Stockton lured people in boats of all sizes and shapes, in sailing ships, in freight wagons and stagecoaches, on foot and on horseback. Often the town was deluged by rain and too often filled with ankle- to knee-deep mud and plagued by mosquitoes. Today we take for granted an absence of mosquitoes, but back then, without any abatement program, residents suffered terribly from clouds of the pests.

Moreover, Stockton was a raw frontier town filled with clutter: empty crates, barrels, mining equipment, pack animals, and abandoned boats. Historian H.H. Bancroft referred to it as a place where gambling, drinking, and dissolute behavior were carried to excess.

Hangings became public spectacles. Later outlaws like Joaquin Murietta and his henchman Manuel "Three-Fingered Jack" Garcia won notoriety, if not inviolability. After they were killed, the head of Murietta and the hand of Garcia were exhibited at the Stockton House, an early hotel. (Recent historical studies claim the head was not Murietta's; so far the hand has escaped scrutiny.)

Weber had participated in the gold search, but after five months he sold his mining company and withdrew to settle in Stockton. He quickly saw his chance for wealth in the roles of merchant and real estate developer. He pioneered the first general store, which flourished. His first ship, the *Maria,* sailed the channel from San Francisco, laden with goods and supplies. Place-names accrued wherever he did business, like Weber's Settlement and Weaver's (a popular mispronunciation) Embarcadero.

Meanwhile the town was growing apace. Weber showed leadership ability in the way he spearheaded development of the town and vision in how he laid out its design by careful plans. He had an eye toward growth and spaciousness: large square blocks, wide streets, standard size lots, and parks. The original city

The 1890 Fourth of July parade, as seen from the courthouse, makes its way along Weber Avenue. Courtesy, Pacific Center for Western Historical Studies, University of the Pacific

Students and teachers of the Franklin Grammar School (also known as Center Street School) pose for a class portrait on the steps of the 1859 brick schoolhouse. Courtesy, Pacific Center for Western Historical Studies, University of the Pacific

of about one square mile was roughly bounded by Flora, Aurora, Edison, and Anderson streets. Later on, the boundaries took in four square miles: Harding to the north, Charter to the south, Wilson to the east, and Pershing to the west. Lots previously considered worthless were selling for hundreds of dollars. On the outskirts, farms were being started by disillusioned gold seekers. By 1851, 600 people were farming within a 10-mile radius of the town.

With his inclination for merchandising and selling, not to mention his capacity for languages (English, German, Spanish, and several Indian dialects), Weber made money quickly. Grotesque inflation reigned throughout the Gold Rush years, whether for bread, pork, boots, tents, or bricks. In 1852 flour cost one dollar a pound, whiskey $30 a quart, and eggs $50 a dozen.

Weber could be tough too. At one time during the early days close to 50 boats were tied up at McLeod Lake and the head of the channel, abandoned by their owners who had scurried off into the hills in search of gold. Swayed by the petition of townfolk, Weber had the boats towed away and burned.

This time of his life, when he was in his thirties, proved significant for Weber in other ways. After marriage to Helen Murphy on November 29, 1850, the couple had two sons, Charles II and Thomas, and a daughter, Julia. Fourteen years after his arrival in America as an immigrant of modest means, Weber had built for his family a mansion at Weber Point, a site overlooking McLeod Lake and the head of the channel. A granite monument now marks its location.

The Webers' one-wing, two-story home of redwood with brick foundation and chimneys and adobe walls became the first substantial dwelling built on the floor of the San Joaquin Valley. According to traveler John McCracken, it cost $300,000, a fortune at the time. A spectacular garden of roses, and many other flowers, was kept irrigated by means of piping run by a steam engine. A thick hedge encircled the grounds, which were occasionally opened to the public.

Weber needed the retreat of his garden to escape thorns of litigation. Squatters had seized much of his land in Stockton and around San Joaquin County, and Weber became embroiled in numerous lawsuits. A major case involving his original land grant led all the way to the Supreme Court. After he finally won patent to this land, the grant was officially signed by Abraham Lincoln in 1861. A note of irony may be detected in the president's acknowledgment of "such a big farm"—his own spread back in Illinois had been only 160 acres.

A hardheaded businessman, Weber could also be compassionate and generous. He gave up his land for streets; he donated 13 park sites, each one block square; he provided the property for a county courthouse, a fire company, the state asylum, and the county fairgrounds, as well as for schools and churches.

In sum, like many a successful entrepreneur, Weber always seemed to be in

Workers unload a barge of bricks at the waterfront while the Masonic Temple (1883-1931) looms behind them. In the 1880s Stockton acquired the nickname "Brick City" because of the many fine brick buildings being constructed. Courtesy, Stockton Public Library

the right place at the right time; often in the face of risk, he made the right decisions; once in a while luck smiled on him. For example: he settled an uninhabited place; the Gold Rush began nearby. He got into financial trouble; astute relatives arrived to help advise him. He could have faced a firing squad; his captor set him free. In addition, he overcame forces of the U.S. government that questioned ownership of his land, he repulsed squatters who occupied his land, and he prevailed over fires and floods and business depressions.

But, as we all do, he lost to his last opponent. Death took Weber unexpectedly at the age of 67 on May 4, 1881, 40 years after his arrival in California. His widow lived at the mansion at Weber Point until three years before her death in 1895. The original home, in ruins, was destroyed by fire in 1917.

The business acumen and hard work that we associate with Weber, combined with the ability to make right decisions in the face of risks, tempered by dashes of good luck, have characterized the careers of other important Stocktonians. These include Benjamin Holt, in a 40-year period to either side of the turn of the century, and Alex Spanos, in a 40-year period at the end of the twentieth century.

Stockton itself succeeded in spite of fires, floods, initially stalled road building, prolonged delays in the dredging of a deeper ship channel, and conflict with the railroads. An early depression occurred when Gold Rush business tailed off badly in the 1850s.

As for fires: a terrible one occurred in 1849, another in 1851, and yet another in 1853. The San Joaquin Fire Engine Company, begun in 1855, helped to extinguish the many blazes to follow, including the loss of a large agricultural pavilion in 1902.

Floods occurred every three or four years, but the worst were in 1847, 1852,

Spectators line the street and lean out windows to watch this patriotic parade. As tractors pulling artillery travel one way, floats, bands, and marchers move in the opposite direction. Courtesy, Pacific Center for Western Historical Studies, University of the Pacific

1861-1862, 1893, 1907, and 1955. The flood of 1847 made the San Joaquin River three miles wide. The overflow in 1861-1862 converted an entire area between Antioch and Stockton into a huge lake; in Stockton flooding went as deep as six feet. In 1907 the entire business district was under water from one to four feet deep. In 1955, seven inches of rain in a short period flooded the southern part of the city. Although Stockton escaped major flooding in 1986, northwestern parts of San Joaquin County were not so fortunate. The building of a diversion canal in 1911, the later construction of dams in the foothills, and levee building have since helped to prevent the severe flooding of the past.

Stockton received its charter as a municipality on July 23, 1850, more than a month before California became a state. Weber himself was selected among the first seven aldermen of the new city. In spite of the presence of rowdy taverns, fandango houses, and general hell-raising, forces of law and conventionality and

In the 1920s and 1930s the Mineral Baths on South San Joaquin Street attracted Stockton residents such as these during hot summer days. The Mineral Baths were eventually renamed McKinley Park and Pool. Courtesy, Pacific Center for Western Historical Studies, University of the Pacific

order prevailed, as they always do. A dozen schools, public and private, were in operation by the 1860s. And the city was illuminated by gas in the 1860s.

A channel-dredging plan surfaced in the late 1860s. In 1870 the Stockton Ship Channel organization formed, but as we shall learn in the next chapter, it took more than 60 years for the dredging to commence.

Stockton had trouble with railroads that were bent on their own self-interest, such as the Southern Pacific. Rail service began in 1869 with the Central Pacific, but not until 20 years later did the Atchison, Topeka, and Santa Fe build a large railroad depot. In 1910, when a third railroad, Western Pacific, joined in, Stockton became the only Western city to be connected by three transcontinental railroads. So, from famine to feast in four decades.

Stockton's population growth has been steady, if not sometimes explosive. We need to remember it was only 1,500 in 1850. Four years later it shot to 7,000, to become the fourth-largest city in California. By 1876, the population had doubled to 14,000. Over the next half-century, growth remained controlled: 23,000 in 1900, 41,000 in 1920, then to the 60,000 range in the 1940s. By the early 1960s, the number had increased to 89,000, and in the quarter-century since, it has more than doubled, to become the 80th-largest city in the United States.

The city's first high school—Stockton High—opened in 1870. Also in the 1870s various kinds of valuable farm equipment were manufactured in Stockton, including a combine harvester. The Stockton Woolen Mills, the California Paper Company, and other industrial plants were then in full swing. The Farmer's

Cooperative Union made agricultural transportation and storage cheaper. Many Chinese, who had worked on railroads, settled in Stockton at this time and established a thriving Chinese community.

In saloons in the 1880s, you could buy a schooner of beer for a nickel, a shot of whiskey for a dime. If you spit tobacco juice at the spitoon and missed, you'd hit sawdust on the floor.

You could get a shave for 15 cents and a bath for a quarter. Stockton was supposed to be the Mudville of Ernest Thayer's poem "Casey at the Bat," which appeared in 1888. The name refers of course to the gooey mud left in Stockton by its frequent rains and flooding.

On the more serious side, in the 1880s Stockton was a leading grain producer in the West. During this period it acquired the name of Brick City because of the many fine brick buildings that were being constructed. One non-brick structure—the aforementioned block-square agricultural pavilion—remained the pride of Central California until the turn of the century when a fire destroyed it. The city was also spreading eastward into the dryland interior.

In the 1890s lots were on sale in North Stockton between Harding Way and Oak Park for a $10 deposit and a dollar per week. In those years door-to-door mail delivery began, the San Joaquin County Courthouse went up, and four

Photographed at City Hall about 1930, members of the Stockton Police Department take inventory of liquor and distilling equipment confiscated during Prohibition. The officer at left (foreground) pours moonshine into a sewer. Courtesy, Pacific Center for Western Historical Studies, University of the Pacific

large flour mills, as well as six banks, were in operation.

Profound changes were by now taking place in Stockton: moving from muddy paths to wooden sidewalks to concrete walks, the city passed into the twentieth century. The horse and buggy gave way to automobiles; streets were filled with electric streetcars and Model Ts. The animal names given by Weber to north-south streets were changed: to Madison (from Beaver), to Monroe (from Elk), to Van Buren (from Bear), to Lincoln (from Otter), to Harrison (from Raccoon). The five sloughs that went deep into the city were gradually filled in. Miner Avenue was once Miner Slough; Hunter Square was built over the old Branch Slough; fill reduced the size of McLeod Lake; and a bridge undergirds Center Street over McLeod Lake.

In 1900 Stockton contained a couple hundred manufacturing companies. The biggest were canneries, boat builders, and manufacturers of farm equipment. Many Italians came to live in Stockton in that first decade. Goods, food, and money were donated to help victims of the San Francisco earthquake in 1906. The number of farms tripled in San Joaquin County, thanks to irrigation.

In 1910 the Hotel Stockton was built in Mission Revival style at the corner of El Dorado and Weber at a cost of $500,000. After some remodeling and partial apportionment into office space, the hotel finally stopped operating in 1960 when it was taken over for county welfare offices. Plans are now under way to restore the building to its former grandeur, possibly as a hotel and office building. A registered landmark, its facade remains a showplace for all of Central California. Several other prominent hotels were also built downtown in that second decade.

World War I produced prosperity for valley farmers, for manufacturers of general goods, and for manufacturers of vehicles used by the military, like the Holt Brothers, who built track-laying tractors to replace artillery-hauling teams of horses and mules. Suburbs spread, including the Tuxedo Park subdivision, Bours Park (an area north of Harding Way on Hunter, San Joaquin, and El Dorado), and also the Victory Park and Yosemite Terrace additions.

The 1920s were marked by some significant occurrences. Approval was gained, both locally and nationally, for widening and deepening the Stockton channel; College of the Pacific (COP) moved to Stockton from San Jose; the Civic Auditorium, City Hall, and the 12-story Medico-Dental Building were constructed; a city manager form of government began in 1923; and two famous riverboats, the *Delta King* and the *Delta Queen*, sternwheelers each almost a block long, were built. Although expansion was going on everywhere in the city, two important businesses—the Holt Manufacturing Company (becoming Caterpillar in a 1925 merger) and Sperry Flour—moved to different parts of the country.

In the midst of the Depression, Stockton managed to hang on. The first phase of the Deep Water Channel was completed, the Fox California Theater was constructed, along with the Pioneer Museum and Haggin Galleries, and the first Hogan Dam was erected up in the foothills. To mark the ever-increasing ethnicity of the city, many Filipinos came to live in Stockton. Before the thirties had run their course, Amos Alonzo (A.A.) Stagg had come to coach football at COP, and Tillie Lewis had started her first cannery.

Obviously World War II dominated Stockton in the 1940s. Eight shipbuilding companies owning 10 shipyards employed 10,000 workers. While shipbuilding

PREVIOUS PAGE: A panoramic view of Stockton in the 1930s shows the growing businesses located downtown. Beneath a magnificent blanket of clouds stands the courthouse (left) and the grandiose Hotel Stockton at the head of the channel. Courtesy, Pacific Center for Western Historical Studies, University of the Pacific

was the leading war industry, airplane parts, weapons, and vehicles were also produced here. The Port of Stockton, Rough and Ready Island, Stockton's airport, and Lathrop's supply facility all became important to the military effort. Japanese-Americans were interned in relocation camps, and a Navy V-12 program was instituted at COP. In the 1940s and into the 1950s, peat dust storms plagued the valley; modern agricultural technology has by now reduced their severity. Finally, two years after the war ended, Stockton's 18 gambling houses were closed.

In 1950 Lincoln Village had only two streets, a couple dozen houses, and no shopping area. Massive expansion followed and has continued to today. In addition, Highway 99 opened on the east side of Stockton, and numerous improvements were made on city streets, including northward extension of Pacific Avenue. Pacific Memorial Stadium (now named for A.A. Stagg) was completed, along with the Stockton Elevators at the Port of Stockton and a huge Diamond Walnut Growers plant (now Sun-Diamond) in East Stockton. Also in the 1950s the building of exclusive homes began in the orchards of Morada northeast of the city limits. Shimizu, Japan, became a sister port city. And downtown's Skid Row, considered one of the largest in the West, prepared to face the wrecker's ball.

BELOW: Errol Flynn fans line up to see Four's a Crowd *at the Fox California theater in the mid-1930s. The theater had a seating capacity of 2,400. Courtesy, Mel Bennett*

In the 1960s Skid Row would all but disappear in the demolition that accompanied urban renewal. Whole blocks of the downtown area were rebuilt, a process continuing into the 1990s. The same holds for expansion of the Stockton Metropolitan Airport. Meanwhile, areas north of the Calaveras River blossomed with new growth. For example, Breuner's moved north to Hammer Lane from a downtown building, and the Weberstown Mall opened in 1966. New retail centers and industrial parks were beginning to spring up everywhere. Varied new buildings were completed, including the San Joaquin County Courthouse, the main library, Burns Tower at UOP, and its striking neighbor, the Central Methodist Church.

The 1970s continued the growth pattern of the previous decade. Retail centers like St. Mark's Plaza, Venetian Square, Quail Lakes, and College Square appeared, coinciding

Colberg Boat Works launches the USS ATR 52 *during the World War II years. In addition to Colberg, the city's other large shipbuilders at the time were Stephen Brothers, Hichenbotham, and the largest—Pollick. Courtesy, Stockton Chamber of Commerce*

with other expansive new development along west March Lane and along north Pershing and Pacific. The same pattern holds for the growth of industrial parks like El Pinal on West Lane.

In compliance with earthquake regulations, many new schools were built; old buildings were torn down, or put to other uses not involving children. Delta College's new campus drew almost 20,000 students. Interstate 5 was completed near Stockton, the final link of a highway system that extends from Latin America to Alaska.

A movement toward controlled growth by voters in the late 1970s faltered somewhat in the 1980s with approval of new housing developments beyond established boundaries. In the meantime Stockton has been building up previously undeveloped land within city limits. Revitalization of the downtown area continues, especially on the waterfront and with completion of the new American Savings Plaza. March Lane, Hammer Lane, and West Lane have undergone further development. New construction also includes the Hilton Hotel and Corn Products Plant, and work continues on the Crosstown Freeway to connect Interstate 5 to Highway 99.

Like the influx of Europeans, Chinese, and Filipinos in earlier decades, the 1980s saw a sharp rise in the immigration of Southeast Asians to Stockton. As the 1990s dawn, Stockton's metropolitan area, bounded roughly on the north by Eight Mile Road and on the south by French Camp Road, to the east by Jack Tone Road and to the west by the Delta, numbers 250,000 residents.

From its beginning, Stockton has moved into the forefront as an agricultural and business center, nexus of transportation service, and a deepwater port.

Early Stockton's near-perfect location and generous farmlands lacked only an avenue of distribution. The opening of the ship channel in 1933 was the final piece of the puzzle and firmly established the city's indispensable role within the region. Photo by Kerrick James

Chapter **3**

Pride in Prosperity

Stockton's triple-header combination of business, agriculture, and shipping has reigned for almost a century and a half. Recently enterprise here has been abetted by a substantial increase in service and transportation industries. Although rail transportation remains important, it has been dwarfed by deep water channel shipping and by highway trucking.

Geographical location has a lot to do with Stockton's expanding role as a distribution center. A transmontane city with coastal ranges on one side and the Mother Lode and Sierra on the other, it's strategically located between two larger Central Valley cities: 45 miles south of Sacramento and 110 miles north of Fresno. Situated along Interstate 5 and Highway 99, Stockton connects Southern California

LEFT: The U.S. Postal Service is one organization that has noticed Stockton's exceptional value as a distribution point. Photo by Kerrick James

FACING PAGE: Miles and miles of rails are among the arteries circulating vital products to and from Stockton. Photo by Steve Pereira

to Central and Northern California and beyond, via a direct line, to Oregon and Washington. Los Angeles is 335 miles to the south; San Francisco 75 miles to the west. Moreover, Stockton lies 180 miles southwest from Reno, and 130 miles in the same direction from Lake Tahoe.

Various companies have recognized Stockton's excellent location as transportation center for the West. For example, J & R Warehouse and Service Company built huge warehouses here to store grocery items to be sold throughout 11 Western states. Honda has a distribution center on the southern outskirts of the city; a huge new U.S. Postal Service Regional Mail Center occupies an expansive parcel of land at Highway 99 and Arch Road adjoining Metropolitan Airport. In all, several million square feet of warehouse space have been built in South Stockton recently. Thirty-five major transcontinental truck lines and another 150 trucking firms are located within the Stockton area.

Stockton has no massive manufacturing plants or factories and no lunch-bucket brigades of workers. While agriculture and food processing remain essential to the local economy, manufacturing has become so widely diversified that close to 400 manufacturing and distribution firms operate in and around the city.

Sun-Diamond, processor and packer of nut products, employs from 450 to a seasonal high of 1,000 workers. The food processing carried on by Del Monte Corporation draws a work force from a low of 250 to a seasonal high of 1,800. California Cedar Products, known for Duraflame Logs and for pencil stock, has 640 employees. Lika Corporation, a division of Tandy that produces printed circuit boards, and American Moulding and Millwork, noted for its lumber products, employ about 400 workers each. Chinchiolo Fruit hires 500; Tri-Valley Growers, 100 to 900; and Ragu Foods, 200 to 450.

Plants employing between 200 and 250 workers include Safeway Meat Processing; J-M Manufacturing, which produces mainly PVC pipe; Stockton Steel (a division of Herrick Corporation), which manufactures steel fabricators; Citation Circuits and Circuit Works, producing printed circuit boards; and Haley Brothers, which makes plywood and structural products. Manufacturers employing a work force of between 100 and 200 include Earth Grains/Merico (wholesale breads and pastries); Apache Plastics (plastic pipe); Parsons of California (aerospace fabrication); Ad-Art (signs); Asco/Delta (electric equipment); Beadex Manufacturing/

Recent expansion at Pacific Avenue's Sherwood Mall is a sign of the times: Stockton's consumers have money to spend. Photo by Steve Pereira

Ameron Pipe (concrete, gypsum, and plaster products); Datura International (communication equipment); Del-Astra (waterbed mattresses); Dopako (paperboard containers and boxes); Holt Brothers (tractors and implements); Stanton Industries (household furniture); Techno Trim, a division of Johnson Controls (seat covers); Gold Bond Building Materials; Monier Roof Tile; and Sierra Lumber Manufacturers.

Non-manufacturing employment accounts for a much larger chunk. San Joaquin County employs almost 3,500 people in the handling of its own administration, and the City of Stockton another 1,400. Almost 2,000 workers report to the corporate headquarters of American Savings Bank, and 1,800 people are employed by St. Joseph's Hospital. Other employers of more than a thousand include Sharpe Army Depot and Pacific Gas and Electric Company. A sampling of other non-manufacturing employers of considerable size includes the Port of Stockton, the General Services Administration (GSA), the *Stockton Record,* Honda, and distributors like Martin-Brower, Foster Farms, O-G Packing, General Potato and Onion, Craig and Hamilton Meats, and Certified Grocers of California. An educational system that ranges from independent University of the Pacific to public San Joaquin Delta College, to public and private secondary, middle, and elementary schools, employs many thousands of teachers and support personnel.

In all, Stockton has more than 10,000 licensed businesses. Eighty percent of them are small businesses. The city opens its arms to new ideas in the marketplace and has a large available labor force to make them work. Dreams still flourish here, and they can become reality. For example:

(1) Less than a decade ago, two women, Angela Franklin and Kathleen Jensen-Jackson, established in Stockton a firm offering various nursing services. Today PRN (Professional Reliable Nursing) services five counties, makes $3 million annually, has 30 office personnel, and employs a field staff of 600. The company has won the Governor's Award for Small Businesses in California and a White House Award from the federal Small Business Administration.

(2) A cosmetologist began with one shop in Stockton. In less than 20 years, Sir Gauuan's has eight salons in Stockton, Lodi, Modesto, and Tracy, and has been given a service industry award by the U.S. Department of Commerce.

(3) In 1981 a handful of partners sized up the need for upscale catering and gourmet foods in Stockton. Installing all the equipment and furnishings themselves, they began a store, with a chic little dining room attached, on Alder Street off Pacific. Now an additional restaurant and a smaller store are in place downtown in the Greenhouse Mall.

(4) Thirty years ago Luther Cozad began making low-bed trailers that haul heavy equipment. He and his staff of three produced one or two trailers a year. Now the firm, operated by Carmelita Cozad, produces 225 low-bed trailers each year. The plant, spread over 10 acres and 90,000 square feet of manufacturing space, employs 55 people. Their custom-made trailers are shipped all over the world.

(5) A UOP chemist left academe to join in business with a former plumber and waterbed salesman turned executive. Their firm of Blue Magic Products

Modern art from an aerial view: up close this becomes a rice paddy. Photo by Mark E. Gibson

employs 110 and has markets around the world for its waterbed chemicals and fittings, household cleaners, and other products.

All enterprises should have such happy endings, but unfortunately they don't. Both the entrepreneurial and the mercurial nature of business is illustrated in the rise and fall of California Cooler on the Stockton scene.

Back in 1981 two boyhood friends from Lodi formed a business out of what they used to do for fun at parties for other friends: mix wine and fruit juices. They started a plant, and sales took off. By 1985 the drink had become the most popular cooler in the nation.

That year the two friends, R. Stuart Bewley and Michael Crete, sold the company to Brown-Forman for $146 million. Fierce competition and ineffective promotion, marketing, and distribution caused sales of California Cooler to plummet over the next couple of years. Rights to the company were then sold to Strohs. The Stockton plant on Tepee Drive that used to employ up to 550 workers closed its doors in early 1989 as production under the new owner moved to Southern California and Tennessee.

Although misfires can occur in agriculture, you'd never know it when you fly over land around Stockton. The beauty of the patchwork quilting, the multi-shapes and multi-colors of so many farms, would please any appreciative eye. Take a Sunday outing in any direction from the city, and you'll equally be impressed by the size of the fields and the variety of crops grown. You can check them out close up by handpicking vegetables and fruits fresh from the fields at roadside stands. Many residents do their shopping at bustling farmers' markets held on weekends at open-air locations around Stockton.

To say that San Joaquin County contains lush farmland is an understatement. Of course, it has the advantage of being in a state that for a long time has placed first among all 50 in the value of its agricultural output.

To be specific, the gross value of California's agricultural production in 1988 was about $13 billion. One of the main contributors to this abundance is the county surrounding Stockton. Presently 870,000 acres of land are under cultivation in San Joaquin County. To put that figure another way, 94 percent of all county land is used for agricultural purposes. The most current census shows 4,500 farms in San Joaquin County, ranging in size from under 10 acres (about a thousand of these) to more than 2,000 acres (65 of them). Most farms are in the 10- to 50-acre size, with the average about 200 acres.

Each year during the late 1980s, San Joaquin County's agricultural output (total gross F.O.B. value) has amounted to three-quarters of a billion dollars. The county has unfailingly ranked sixth, seventh, or eighth in the nation in the value of its agricultural production. Moreover, agriculture pumps $3.7 billion annually into the county's economy.

The latest annual figures for San Joaquin County's leading agricultural products, in order, show: milk (12 million cwt), grapes (49,000 acres), almonds (36,000 acres), cherries (7,000 acres), tomatoes (25,000 acres), walnuts (25,000 acres), eggs (92 million dozen), cattle and calves (160,000 head), sugar beets (37,000 acres), and hay (65,000 acres).

San Joaquin County yields 80 farm products. Other major field crops, below the top 10, are dry beans, corn, rice, safflower, wheat, and sunflowers. Major vegetable crops other than tomatoes include asparagus, peppers, cucumbers, onions,

melons, and potatoes. Besides the fruit and nut crops listed in the top 10, apricots and peaches also rank high in total yield. Bulbs and turf, flowering potted and foliage plants, and woody ornamentals are among the county's nursery products. Major livestock, dairy, and poultry following the top 10 include chickens, turkeys, sheep and lambs, hogs and pigs, and wool. And let's not forget those busy honey bees that bring in almost $2 million annually.

Most urbanites are surprised that the region's leading farm product is milk. More than a hundred dairy farms rack up almost $140 million worth of production each year. As expected, San Joaquin County's second largest crop is its great variety of grapes. The total value of 1988's crop was $61 million. The region's prime vineyards produce Chardonnay, Cabernet sauvignon, zinfandel, sauvignon blanc, chablis, burgundy, and popular table wines. Visitors may take tours and taste wines at many local wineries, among them Delicato Vineyards in Manteca and Guild Wineries in Lodi.

About one-fourth of California's crops are shipped out of state. For example, fruits and vegetables go to the East Coast, cherries to Japan, walnuts and almonds to Europe. Asparagus has been shipped around the country since 1900 and around the world for several decades.

The Stockton farming area is famous for its asparagus, a vegetable of great

ABOVE: Local residents pick the best of the best when it comes to produce for their own tables. Photo by Steve Pereira

FACING PAGE: According to recent figures, cherries account for roughly 7,000 acres of local farmland, making them a leading agricultural product. Photo by Bo Richards

appeal: crisp, well textured, and tasty. Currently in San Joaquin County the asparagus cultivated on about 18,000 acres has a market value of $23 million. California as a state produces about three-fourths of the nation's supply of asparagus, and, as it has since the 1850s, most of that amount comes from the Delta.

As early as 1849, Bayard Taylor argued for embankment for the Delta and predicted that agriculture would make it "one of the most beautiful and productive portions of the nation." The reclamation took many decades. Thousands of workers, most of them Chinese and Mexican, helped to build levees to create island upon island of peat land, much of the soil below sea level, and all of it extremely productive. This land has been subjected to floods and other vicissitudes of nature.

Progress, too, has made its claims upon natural beauty. Many tens of thousands of valley oaks were cut down to make way for grain fields. The same fate

LEFT: Pistachios are among the many nut crops cultivated in the area. Photo by John Elk III

FACING PAGE, TOP: California has been the nation's green grocer for a long time, and "California's Cornucopia" is responsible for much of that bounty. Photo by Steve Pereira

FACING PAGE, BOTTOM: Though Stockton's acres of patchwork fields are highly conspicuous, the region's leading farm product is actually milk. Some of it is dried and transported out the channel to India. Photo by Steve Pereira

overtook field crops and orchards in the path of housing developments. Gary W. Johnston, San Joaquin County extension director, worries about irreplaceable loss of farmland. "Every 500 acres that disappears to a housing project is land that cannot be replaced," he says. "We need to think about the consequences of this conversion. Besides lost land, think of the ecosystem that can't be duplicated." But Johnston remains optimistic about agriculture and sees it remaining a major force in the county's economy for a long time to come.

Besides the richness of surrounding agricultural lands, another key to Stockton's development has been the dredging of the Stockton channel. The deepening of the channel to accommodate ocean-going vessels took 63 years from inception to fruition. The initial dredging took only a couple of years; argument and delay ate up all the rest. And the deepening continues to this day.

In the early years following the founding of Stockton, only shallow-draft boats could transport cargo. In 1870 the Stockton Ship Channel Company formed in the hope of bringing in deeper draft vessels. Channel enthusiasts were discouraged by the dredging costs, and then a drought the following year further dimmed their plans. In 1874 the proposal resurfaced, only to be dropped once again. The ensuing years brought considerable opposition from Sacramento and from Bay Area cities threatened by a prospective loss of trade. Other obstacles like fog, flooding, and concern over the protection of water fowl impeded progress on the channel.

A big enterprise fails to deter a small one, as two local fishermen go about catching some dinner. Photo by Steve Pereira

In 1901 a congressional committee visited the channel, and in 1906 Joseph N. Ransdell, a congressman from Louisiana, took up the cry "15 feet to the sea." From 1908 to 1910 a channel was dug to divert water from Mormon Channel back into the Calaveras east of Stockton, but the diversion was just that—a diversion.

Next, World War I intervened. Nothing of any significance happened until 1919 when Army Engineers, who were also in favor of the channel, raised the figure to "24 feet to the sea." Another six years went by before the chief of the Army Engineers approved a recommendation for a depth of 30 feet. In April of that same year, 1925, Stockton passed, by an overwhelming majority of 13 to 1, a Deep Water Bond to raise $3 million. In 1927 President Calvin Coolidge signed the bill, and in 1930 the city received its first payment of $365,000 for the project.

Sixty-one years after the idea was first proposed, work on the channel actually began, both to deepen and to widen it. The stretch from Sui-

The 1906 rallying cry of "Fifteen feet to the sea" became more ambitious over the years, resulting in a channel 37 feet deep at average low tide. Photo by Kerrick James

sun Bay to Stockton ran 41 miles. Peat, alluvium, soft clay, tule roots, sand, and gravel amounting to more than 20 million cubic yards were removed by two different kinds of dredges (and then used to shore up Delta levees). Also, the natural oxbow river bends had to be eliminated, and the turning basin had to be improved.

The ship channel officially opened in 1933 when the *Daisy Gray* made its way into Stockton with 700,000 board feet of lumber. Never let it be said that the wheels of bureaucracy move swiftly. But for Stockton, persistence paid off.

Dredging has continued from the 1930s into the late 1980s. The channel is now at a depth of 37 feet at average low tide. It can accommodate up to 55,000-ton class ships, maximum 60,000 class for some wide-beam vessels, and up to 80,000-ton class vessels partially loaded. There are no width restrictions, but maximum length is 900 feet, or twice the length of an average-sized cargo ship. (For example, a World War II Victory ship was 455 feet long.) Obviously certain contemporary vessels, such as supertankers that draw twice as much water as present channel depth, will never darken our piers. Maybe just as well, since these behemoths were built for ocean and gulf travel.

The Port itself has been steadily renovated and improved for more than 50 years. It now contains 10 separate piers. The Port has added warehouses, bulk storage facilities, cranes, conveyors, elevators, an oil terminal, pneumatic piping, and

bulk silos. Other facilities include a rotary rail car dump and loop railroad for handling unit trains. The Port handles coal, petroleum coke, sulfur, copper concentrates, and other bulk commodities, in addition to containers and other general cargoes.

Over a 7- to 10-hour period, ships make their way from the Golden Gate via San Pablo Bay, the Carquinez Strait, and Suisun Bay into the winding San Joaquin River. By 1988 almost 13,000 ships had visited Stockton. The Port imports about 90 products and exports about 120. Moreover, the Port has been, on average, the largest employer in the city over the past half-century.

In busy times at the Port, nine ships will load or unload industrial or agricultural cargo. Among cargoes delivered during a recent month were steel beams and steel coils from Japan, liquid ammonia from Canada, and powdered fertilizer from Europe; cargoes loaded during the same period were dried milk for India and wheat for Central America. A major part of the Port's trade involves Western Europe, India, and countries along the twin arcs of the Pacific Rim from Australia to Korea, primarily Japan, and from Chile to northernmost Mexico.

The Port is a major landlord; 50 tenants lease some of its 600 acres and construct and operate their own facilities. Also, as part of the channel project, the Port constructed two wetland habitats for fish and wildlife, one at Donlan Island in Sacramento County and the other at Venice Cut Island in San Joaquin County. Both islands are to be maintained by the Port into perpetuity.

In summary, Professor Nicholas P. Hardeman has written movingly on this harbor of the heartlands:

> *Stockton is the Pacific port with the personal, rural touch. Observant merchant mariners recognize it as a port with a difference. Where else does one reach sheltering harbor by gliding along an aisle lined with mossy-trunked oaks, elms, and cottonwoods richly plumed with dark clumps of mistletoe? Where the hawk stares statue-like from its perch, and gaudy red-winged blackbirds clamor in the tule and cattail fringes of gently flowing current? Great blue herons stand motionless, silhouetted against glassy backgrounds, and colorful ringnecked pheasants dart along grass-covered levees. An occasional beaver paddles homeward with its own cargo. It is a restful scene, a blend of the very old with the new, of the modern and mechanized with the wild and primitive, as surely as it is a setting where land arteries embrace sea lanes in bustling commerce.*

Aside from the Port, the Waterfront area brims with activity and growth. At the instigation of SDI Developers, renovation and building proceeded for a time on the south shore. Planned development of the north shore and continued work on the south shore are in the offing. It appears that HKM Associates will spearhead these projects. The Waterfront remains an attraction to varied businesses, including the Colberg and Stephens boat building families.

Among attractive buildings in the Waterfront area is the Warehouse, an outstanding example of architecture surviving from the nineteenth century. Beginning in 1870 local farmers stored their grain there, under the aegis of the Grangers Cooperative Union. Twenty years later Sperry and Company expanded the Warehouse and next to it constructed the largest flour mill ever built in the

FACING PAGE: Improvement of the channel has continued for decades; today all but the largest vessels can pull up to the Port of Stockton. Photo by Steve Pereira

FACING PAGE: Stockton's persistence in developing the ship channel has paid great dividends for both the economy and lifestyle of the entire region. Photo by Steve Pereira

BELOW: The Port has grown and modernized as the channel has deepened, adding new piers, storage facilities, and equipment for optimal handling of both bulk and containerized cargoes. Photo by Steve Pereira

Central Valley. By the 1940s, the building contained a wholesale grocery warehouse and a sign business. In 1980 SDI renovated the building and converted it into retail stores, restaurants, and offices that include the local chamber of commerce.

The Sheraton Corporation has proposed construction of a major new hotel next to the Warehouse. If approved, completion of the project, to include a city-built parking garage, is expected in the early 1990s. At its early stage, the plan remains no more than speculation.

Any Stocktonian or visitor who witnesses a choice sunset from the Waterfront is in for a treat. The sequined waters and the emerging silhouettes of many moored boats along the Marina evoke pleasure and tranquility.

Back to business. The spread of retail stores around the city, especially to the north, shows continuing commercial expansion. Some two dozen major retail shopping centers have sprung up, led by two malls on Pacific Avenue. The Weberstown Mall is the larger with 825,000 square feet of retail space and near 100

percent capacity at 75 stores. Its large anchor stores include Weinstock's, J.C. Penney, Sears, and nearby Circuit City. Neighboring Sherwood Mall, recently expanded to include Gottschalks's on the east side, also features Montgomery Ward and Macy's at its north and south sides.

Stockton's two largest shopping plazas are Lincoln Center, north and south of Benjamin Holt off Pacific, and College Square, at Pershing and March. Lincoln Center contains some 60 stores, more than a dozen restaurants, and 30 service-oriented businesses, while College Square features Mervyn's and Best.

Some other shopping areas include St. Mark's Plaza, Quail Lakes, and Venetian Gardens along March Lane, and Hammer Ranch, Normandy Village, and West Lane Plaza along Hammer Lane. Two big discount outlets, Costco and Home Club, have also set up on Hammer Lane, in unadorned warehouse-like buildings, each covering more than 100,000 square feet.

Downtown and older Stockton have not been ignored in the process. The Greenhouse in the center of the city is an attractive assemblage of small shops. Business has remained steady for varied merchants along Charter Way to the south, as it has on the "Miracle Mile," a stretch of stores along Pacific Avenue that began expanding in the 1940s.

A key to the development of these service-related retail stores that annually top $1 billion in sales has been the expansion of housing in Stockton. Houses here sell for about one-third to two-thirds below housing in dense population centers of the state, particularly in Los Angeles, Orange County, and the Bay Area. Thus, affordability becomes a major advantage, translating into savings for Stockton home buyers of $60,000 to $135,000 for comparable homes elsewhere. According to the California Association of Realtors, a single-family home in late 1988 cost $226,000 on the average in such cities as Anaheim and Santa Ana in Orange County, $214,000 in San Francisco, $191,000 in Los Angeles, and $152,000 in San Diego. By comparison, the average price for a single family home in Stockton is $95,000.

In all Stockton contains about 72,000 homes, including 45,000 single-family units. The housing varies in styles from modest flat-topped bungalows to gabled, roomy two-story Victorians to identical rows of condos to million-dollar-plus

The channel is now open to vessels up to the 55,000-ton class—in some cases even larger—and to vessels as long as 900 feet. Photo by Steve Pereira

custom homes. A charming feature of the older neighborhoods—unlike most new developments—is the distinctly different architectural styles of the homes.

Still, new homes are needed. Over the last five years an average of 635 single-family homes and 800 multiple-family dwellings have been built in the city. Coincidentally, three of the nation's largest home builders—Grupe Company, A.G. Spanos, and Robertson Homes—are headquartered in Stockton.

Businesses moving here from elsewhere have taken advantage of cheaper land costs. For instance, Toys 'R' Us and Fresh Start Bakery from San Jose, J & R from Hayward, and Laser Light from Palo Alto discovered that they could relocate to Stockton, buy property at a fraction of the cost, avoid congestion, and still service the Bay Area from which they came.

Medical costs and coverage also figure importantly in the profile of a city. The largest medical/surgical hospital between Sacramento and Fresno is St. Joseph's, in operation in Stockton since 1898. It contains more than 300 beds, a regional cancer center, and new outpatient facilities. The oldest is San Joaquin General, a large public hospital of more than 230 beds on a 430-acre site south of the city off Interstate 5. It has had a distinguished history since the Civil War as a public facility and as a teaching hospital.

Another large private hospital in addition to St. Joseph's is Dameron. In terms of potential expansion, Dameron is disadvantageously situated in an established residential neighborhood in Central Stockton. It has a well-known advanced burn center and a new cardiovascular department. A fourth addition to the area's hospitals is Kaiser Permanente, a large complex in a new location at Hammer and West Lane.

The State Hospital of Stockton also has a long history. It began in 1851 on 100 acres of land donated by Charles Weber. Over many years it operated at its California Street location, along with a farm producing much of its food at a site now occupied by Delta College. For a long time it suffered from overcrowded conditions during which the population of mental patients climbed from 1,000 to 4,500. Now service has been drastically reduced as more clients are treated as outpatients. Now known as the Stockton Developmental Center and still under the operation of the State of California, the facility has been redesigned into smaller, more attractive units.

Besides many available convalescent homes, almost 250 board and care homes provide services for about 3,000 people. These residents need help caring for themselves, though they're not debilitated enough to be in convalescent hospitals. A final health care statistic worth noting: Stockton provides 142 doctors for every 100,000 residents.

Changes have been dramatic at the Stockton Metropolitan Airport, which is owned and operated by San Joaquin County. In addition to flight service by USAir and United Express, the airport provides airplane, helicopter, charter, and courier/freight services, major car rentals, and unlimited free parking. The airport, located to the southeast of the city, is large enough at a runway length of 8,650 feet to accommodate big jets.

All this growth and development could not have occurred if Stockton had not had its fair share of movers and shakers. Certainly Benjamin Holt is among those leaders. Born in New Hampshire in 1849, Holt moved to California with

The nineteenth-century Warehouse building has been given new life in recent years, and may soon be joined next door by a major hotel. Photo by Kerrick James

A bronze wash of twilight paints the channel in one of its more contemplative moods. Photo by Steve Pereira

his brother Charles, and in 1883 they established the Stockton Wheel Company. From wheels and wagon parts they branched out into the manufacturing of farm machinery. Ben was an inveterate inventor who loved to work with vehicles, machine parts, and tools, and he never minded grease and dirt. An admirer of Edison (he even named a son after him), Holt is sometimes referred to as the Edison of the West.

The Holt brothers sought to produce machines that could cut and thresh and clean wheat, in the face of Central California's tremendous wheat production. During this time California ranked sixth among states in wheat production. For instance, in 1882 San Joaquin County produced 4 million bushels of wheat. So Holt and his associates worked to perfect a link belt combine harvester that could be operated on side hills as well as on flat terrain. Earlier models, which operated with gears, were troubled by mechanical problems.

The link belt, though, did the trick. Engineer Roy Bainer has claimed that the combine harvester is "the most important agricultural invention of the last 300 years."

The machine was also easy to operate. To illustrate the point and the Holt Company's flair for "PR," in 1895 four young women took control of a combine harvester drawn by 26 horses. One woman guided the horses, the second tended the header, the third took charge of the sack sewer, and the fourth operated the separator. While this publicity stunt was intended to demonstrate ease of operation then, today it would merely show that women are as capable as men in operating heavy equipment.

New inventive challenges lay ahead for Holt. He needed to be able to produce machines that could operate in soft, rich peat soil without constantly sinking. To meet this specific demand he and his associates perfected a track-type or crawler tractor—which came to be called the Caterpillar when Holt's photographer remarked that it looked like the insect in the way it put down, moved, and picked up its own base.

Stockton is a good place to settle down, with houses selling for less than half the price of homes in Los Angeles or San Francisco. Photo by Steve Pereira

The machines became more complicated as Holt and his co-workers pressed on with their inventiveness. Their Caterpillar track-type tractor was first steam driven, then gas operated, in increasingly ingenious designs. The Holts' Stockton manufacturing plant in 1900 covered an eight-square block area. They later expanded their operation to Walla Walla and to Peoria.

Aside from his prowess as an inventor, Holt proved to be a first-rate entrepreneur. His firm had the material resources, financial capital, technology, management skills, and the markets and means of transportation to make its endeavors successful. By 1915, 2,000 Holt units were being used in 20 countries around the world. When World War I erupted, the track-laying tractor was used to replace horses in hauling supplies and artillery for the armies of the U.S.,

Main Street exemplifies the overall Stockton ambience: green and pleasant, yet enjoying a lively business climate. Photo by Mark E. Gibson

A brisk housing market, Stockton is home to three of the nation's leading home builders and sees hundreds of new homes go up each year. Older, more established neighborhoods are yet another facet of the city. Photo by Steve Pereira

Air shows are a major attraction at Stockton's airport. Here, viewers mill around an Air Force transport plane. Photo by Kerrick James

Great Britain, France, and Russia. Ten thousand machines were produced by companies either owned or licensed by Holt and obviously had a tremendous impact on World War I, especially when the Caterpillar tracks were adapted to new usage by the British for a military tank. One can imagine how Holt felt when he saw his gas-powered track-laying tractor transformed into an armored combat vehicle. During the war the Holt plant in Stockton employed between 2,500 and 4,000 workers at an annual payroll of $2.5 million.

Holt died in Stockton in 1920, three weeks shy of his 72nd birthday, leaving his widow, the former Anna Brown. The couple had four sons and a daughter, all raised in Stockton at the family residence at 548 East Park. The home is still standing.

This accomplished inventor, manufacturer, and entrepreneur remained modest to the end of his days. His outstanding contribution, according to Reynold M. Wik, was "the development of the first successful track type farm tractor, which later served as a prototype for the military tank, the bulldozer, and other track-laying machinery."

After a 1925 merger with the Best Tractor Company of San Leandro, the entire Holt operation moved to Peoria, where Caterpillars are still manufactured today.

Robert LeTourneau followed the same path as Holt. A valley resident who

Morning fog lends a secluded feel to a house on Smith's Canal. Photo by Mark E. Gibson

invented and promoted various kinds of scrapers and earth-moving equipment, LeTourneau eventually moved his production company to the Midwest. His company later combined with and became absorbed by Westinghouse.

Meanwhile, the memory of Ben Holt lingers on: a main thoroughfare in Lincoln Village is named after him; collections of his machines may be found in the Pioneer Museum and the San Joaquin County Historical Museum, and his family members left a lasting imprint upon the University of the Pacific and its library.

Aside from Holt and founder Charles Weber, Stockton has produced many other leaders who have had a profound effect upon the city and its environs. Some examples, in brief:

(1) Lodowick U. Shippee (1824-1896), born in Rhode Island, a rancher, merchant, financier, and horse breeder. He was one of the founders of the Bank of Stockton, founder of the Stockton Gravel Company, and head of the Stockton Combined Harvest Agriculture Works.

(2) Rufus B. Lane (1831-1907) arrived in Stockton in 1850 from Maine. He became a businessman, flour mill operator, paper maker, and mayor.

(3) Thomas Cunningham (1838-1900) became the most famous lawman of his time in Central California. He served as sheriff of San Joaquin County for 27 years and was widely known as a humanitarian.

(4) James H. Budd (1851-1908) remains to this day the only Stockton resident to be elected governor. A Democrat, he took office in 1894, after serving as second district congressman in 1882.

(5) George Shima (1863-1926), an immigrant from Japan, mastered the recla-

mation and planting of land. From 1890 to his death he planted many thousands of acres of Delta land with potatoes and other vegetables such as asparagus and onions. He became known as the "Potato King" of the Delta.

(6) Tillie Lewis (1901-1977) began Tillie Lewis Foods in 1935. Her canneries, Stockton's largest, produced six million cases of canned foods annually. She was selected U.S. Businesswoman of the Year in 1952. Known for backing charitable causes, she purportedly started her multi-million-dollar business with some seeds and $10,000.

(7) Warren Atherton (1892-1976), known as author of the GI Bill of Rights, was a Stockton attorney. He became national commander of the American Legion and a supporter of many historical and cultural activities, including leadership of the Opera Association. With William Knox Holt, he is responsible for the Holt-Atherton Pacific Center for Western Studies.

(8) Alex G. Spanos (born 1923), of Greek heritage, started out in the 1950s selling food and beverages to workers from a truck; as 1990 dawns he has housing construction projects throughout the U.S. In the fall of 1988, *Forbes* estimated his worth at $550 million. Controlling owner of the San Diego Chargers, Spanos is a respected benefactor of UOP, hospitals, and many charities.

Other leaders include black educator Jeremiah B. Sanderson, orphanage and hospital founder Julia Weber, architect Charles Beasley, flour king Austin Sperry, college president Tully C. Knoles, city manager Elder Gunter, and activists Dario Marenco and the Reverend Robert Green. Furthermore, every year since 1955, a person contributing most in community service and civic activities has been selected as "Stocktonian of the Year" (see Appendix). More such leaders will come along, of course, as Stockton's business community continues to expand. The city's Office of Economic Development, headed by Dave Schmidt, has been instrumental in spurring growth in the commercial and manufacturing sectors. A 25-member citizen's advisory group, appointed by the city council, works to create new jobs and to attract investors. The Greater Stockton Chamber of Commerce works assiduously for the economic development of the city. In addition, the Private Industry Council, consisting of business representatives, educators, and community leaders from throughout San Joaquin County, is also working to develop new jobs and to assist new businesses with start-up support.

So the economic climate in Stockton is, in a word, healthful. The boom may not be extra loud, but it has been good and steady.

From the city itself to the land around it, Stockton is a good place to look for room to move, room to breathe, and room to grow. Photo by Steve Pereira

ABOVE: The far-seeing eye of Stockton founder Charles Weber looks out from a wall in the historical district. The city's history has been enriched by leaders in every field from education to politics. Photo by Steve Pereira

RIGHT: If there wasn't a Stockton, California would have to invent one: this is a city with many jobs to do, and a proven ability to do them. Photo by Steve Pereira

Since 1926 the Stockton Symphony has performed a repertoire to fill the house during its season, which lasts from September through May. Photo by Steve Pereira

Chapter 4

Spirit So Profound

Culture thrives in Stockton. Educational institutions here merit excellent rankings. And plenty of community activities, sports, and leisure-time diversions are readily available for everyone to enjoy.

Theater and entertainment have done well in Stockton since its early days, when the city was visited by the likes of Sarah Bernhardt, Will Rogers, and Al Jolson. Circuses, Wild West shows, operas, plays, and musicals were all popular. More recently, resident and visiting performers have provided audiences with memorable moments: Shelley Berman swaggering as flashy Nathan Detroit in *Guys and Dolls;* Patricia Morrison affectionately gathering her royal pupils around her to sing "Getting to Know You" in *The King and I;* Audree O'Connell scheming as

ABOVE: Housed inside the Pioneer Museum is Haggin Galleries. A plethora of classic art works, including nineteenth-century American and French pieces, inspire viewers. Photo by Kerrick James

FACING PAGE: Victory Park is home to the city's Pioneer Museum, which provides Stocktonians with a view of the area's past. Photo by Kerrick James

Menotti's Medium; and Franklin Wilbur ranting as a bereft King Lear.

Often a region's commitment to culture may be measured by its commitment to theater. Stockton's is commendable. The Stockton Civic Theater, going on its 40th year, produces almost a dozen plays and musicals a year. Its compact, modern theater is located in Venetian Square. Both the University of the Pacific and Delta College run vigorous drama programs. Fans of old-time melodrama who like to hiss the villain can attend a dinner theater at the Pollardville Western Village north of the city.

Outlying theaters are also active, such as the Tokay Players in Lodi and the Manteca Community Theater. Or theatergoers can take a pleasant hour's drive up into the scenic Mother Lode to see plays staged by either of two flourishing repertory companies. The outstanding Sierra Repertory Theatre in Sonora offers a full calendar of seven productions year round. Originally begun by former UOP students, Sierra Rep has entered its second decade. The newer Columbia Actors Repertory at Fallon House Theatre in Columbia State Park offers six productions from September through May. Neither theater is large, but both frequently play to packed houses. Brighter magnitude stars beckon from elsewhere, too, like the Music Circus in Sacramento, Berkeley Rep, and professional theater in San Francisco.

All during the summertime months, drama continues at Delta College, Stockton Civic Theater, Lincoln High School, and throughout the city, under the auspices of a special City Parks and Recreation program. All of them offer a full complement of plays, musicals, and children's productions. Each summer, too, some 20 UOP students undergo a demanding experience when they work and perform in five repertory productions at Fallon House.

The history of Fallon House extends back to the post-Gold Rush era. Beginning as a dance hall in the 1860s and fulfilling other purposes along the way, it became a theater in the 1880s. UOP (then College of the Pacific) purchased the property in 1943, and two years later deeded the theater building and grounds to the state. The college began its summer repertory program at Fallon House in 1954 and continued it there for nearly three decades. Bats nested in the old building; sometimes they flew about in the midst of performances. During a two-year hiatus in the early 1980s, the state restored and modernized the building. Since then, Columbia Rep and UOP have shared the theater—sans bats.

No matter your tastes in theater—whether for serious drama like *Hedda Gabler* or *Death of a Salesman,* for comedy like *The Odd Couple* or *Steel Magnolias,* or for musical productions running the gamut from *The Three-Penny Opera* to

The simple yet elegant layout of the Haggin Galleries creates an ideal forum for the display of many traditional works. Photo by Kerrick James

Little Shop of Horrors—they will be satisfied. The above list offers merely a few samples of productions staged in and around Stockton during the past year.

Stockton maintains a first-rate museum, the Pioneer, which houses the Haggin Galleries, in Victory Park. The Pioneer, which opened in 1931, features nineteenth-century American and French art, from Albert Bierstadt's sweeping landscapes of Yosemite Valley to Adolphe William Bouguereau's naked nymphs in forest glades. The museum also displays artifacts from two centuries of history, including a huge, green and red Haines-Hauser combine harvester (made by Holt Manufacturing in 1904), pulled by a Holt "75" Caterpillar track-type tractor (circa 1918). The popular Annual National Print and Drawing Exhibition, sponsored by the Stockton Arts Commission, draws artists across the country, and 10 times more of their work than can be shown. A designated judge selects outstanding works as Purchase Awards, which are later exhibited under the Arts Commission's Art in Public Places program.

Two different art commissions serve the area. The Stockton Arts Commission, consisting of nine members each serving a four-year term, is appointed by the city council. The San Joaquin County Arts Council, a 14-member board, contributes to the arts in cities and towns throughout the county beyond Stockton.

A treasury of artifacts reflecting the county's past may also be seen at the San Joaquin County Historical Museum on the grounds of Micke Grove Park, north of the city. The Alan Short Gallery on East Acacia features a folk art shop and a gallery that shows the work of contemporary local and nationally known artists. Once the superintendent's residence at the former State Hospital, the building, a white-columned, southern-style mansion erected in 1900, has been declared a historic landmark. Also, several private galleries dot the city.

Whether the Sugar Plum Fairy pirouetting across a twinkling stage, a huge chorus lifting its one voice in song, or violins flashing in unison through a Beethoven concerto, the arts abound in Stockton. Indeed, musical, choral, and dance groups play a prominent part in the city's cultural life. The Stockton Symphony, founded in 1926 and the fifth-oldest orchestra in California, attracts full houses during its September through May season. (Each performance is given over two successive nights.) Also worthy of note are the San Joaquin Concert Ballet; the Stockton Chorale, which has toured Europe; the Stockton Opera Association, now in its 20th year; the UOP A Cappella Choir; and community groups such as Ballet Folkorico Del Puerto and Otea Marinatha Polynesia. Additionally, the Stockton Community Concert Association and the Friends of Chamber Music bring in distinguished performers.

At the Memorial Civic Auditorium in downtown Stockton, boxers jab and counterpunch over the same floor where elegantly gowned and tuxed dancers glided

FOLLOWING PAGE, TOP AND BOTTOM: All kinds of events take place for the Stockton community at the city's Memorial Civic Auditorium, adorned with flowing fountains and guarded by the ever-vigilant California Grizzly. Photos by Mark E. Gibson

BELOW: A Holt combine, towed by an earlier Holt tractor, dates from the early part of the century and stands as a tribute to Central Valley agriculture at the Pioneer Museum. Photo by Kerrick James

the previous evening during a symphony ball. This all-purpose building, which seats 3,616, is also used for banquets, exhibitions, conventions, public addresses, theater and concert productions, circuses, and basketball games.

Three distinctive buildings on the UOP campus figure prominently in community life. The Alex G. Spanos Center seats more than 6,000 and hosts basketball and volleyball games, as well as other sporting events and concerts. The newly renovated mauve and green, 1,200-seat Faye Spanos Concert Hall and the 460-seat Long Theater are used for the performing arts, lectures, and special events. Performers appearing recently at the university have included Bob Hope, Diahann Carroll and Vic Damone, Kenny Loggins, Alabama, the Kronos Quartet, Cyndi Lauper, Reba McIntyre, Sammy Davis, Jr., and rock groups such as Jefferson Starship, Berlin, and the Pretenders. On the Delta campus, the

stately 2,000-seat Atherton Auditorium hosts celebrities, concerts, and large-scale musical productions. The adjoining 300-seat Tillie Lewis Theater is available for smaller productions, including children's theater.

The city also boasts 50 parks (5 of them with community centers), 25 playgrounds, 15 movie theaters, 5 golf courses, 70 tennis courts, 30 softball diamonds, 5 municipal and 18 community swimming pools, and an ice skating rink.

The rainbowed gates of Pixie Woods, a children's park at Louis Park near the channel, have beckoned to nearly 2 million visitors since 1954, when the park was founded. Admission fees are reasonable for its many attractions, including a ride on a miniature mine train and a trip on a paddlewheel steamer. The park's fairy-tale settings feature animals and playgrounds and puppet shows at the Toadstool Theater. The "three little pigs" are replaced regularly as they outgrow their houses of straw, twigs, and brick. Pixie Woods is open intermittently during the spring and fall and daily during the summer, from June through September.

University of the Pacific's Alex G. Spanos Center, named for Stockton's premier developer/philanthropist, plays host to the school's basketball and volleyball games, in addition to other significant school events. Photo by Mark E. Gibson

Micke Grove Park, located 10 miles north of Stockton on 60 acres of tall, shady valley oaks, contains a zoo, an amusement center, picnic and play areas in well-manicured lawns, a Japanese garden, and the San Joaquin County Historical Museum. The other major regional park is Oak Grove, off Freeway 5 at Eight Mile Road, which has 167 acres of oaks and nature trails as well as a lake.

A number of movies and TV shows have been filmed in Stockton and its environs. Stockton's film career began in 1920 at Dad's Point (now Louis Park) with the shooting of *The Jack Knife Man* by the King Vidor Company and at Mormon Slough with *The Whistle* starring William S. Hart. On the Delta John Ford directed America's beloved philosopher-wit Will Rogers in 1935 as a steamboat captain in *Steamboat Round the Bend.* Since then, probably a hundred full-length features, portions of movies, TV episodes, and commercials have been filmed in and around Stockton.

Given California's many attractions, tourism is the second-largest industry in the state, annually providing one-half million jobs and generating $2 billion in state and local taxes. It's estimated that income from tourism in San Joaquin County totals a modest $3 million a year.

Stockton itself has few attractions to draw tourists from afar. However, it does hold events that attract visitors from San Joaquin and surrounding counties. Thousands of residents volunteer as aides for these events. Stocktonians are quite independent of mind, but a genuine sense of community does grip them when certain festivals occur around the city.

Cut to a balmy summer night in the valley, a black sky lit by multicolored fireworks reflecting off water and accompanied by "oohs" and "aahs" from tens

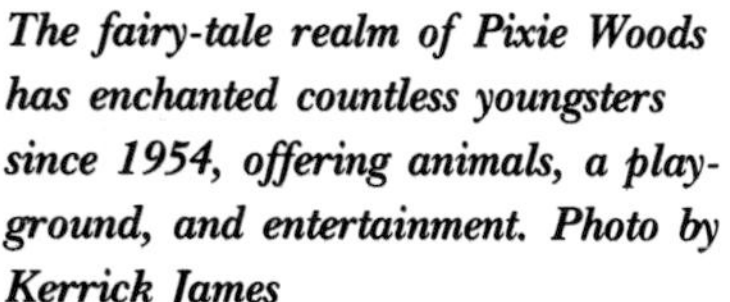

The fairy-tale realm of Pixie Woods has enchanted countless youngsters since 1954, offering animals, a playground, and entertainment. Photo by Kerrick James

of thousands of upturned faces, and you have the annual Waterfest, held on July 3 and July 4. In addition to a climactic fireworks display, the Waterfest features concerts, a yacht parade, and boat rides. McLeod Lake and the Waterfront area provide the festival's downtown setting. Backed by 50 sponsors, the Waterfest attracts some 100,000 spectators.

LEFT AND BELOW: Every May, Stockton Metropolitan Airport offers airplane aficionados an airshow, featuring fearless fliers, skydivers, and historic aircraft. Photos by Steve Pereira

In late May an airshow held at the Stockton Metro Airport draws at least 70,000. The event features flying demonstrations, skydiving, exhibits of aviation history, and displays of airplanes and aviation equipment.

The Asparagus Festival, which takes place at Oak Grove Park, has counted upward of 60,000 spectators and participants. Held over a weekend in April, it features sale of the valley's famed asparagus—straight up or in some rather amazing concoctions—along with entertainment on varied stages, exhibitions of vintage automobiles, arts and crafts booths, and special programs for children.

NEW YORK

Proceeds go to nonprofit community organizations.

Stockton's ethnic diversity has generated a number of festivals. These include Cinco de Mayo, Black History Week, Martin Luther King Day, the Greek Food Fair, Jewish Food Festival, (Japanese) Oban Festival, Filipino Barrio Festival, Chinese New Year's Festival, and International Friendship Day, a food festival at the Civic Auditorium.

Other cultural events held in the city include an Arts Recognition Dinner and an Agribusiness Show in January, the San Joaquin Home and Garden Show and a Cherry Blossom Festival in April, the San Joaquin County Fair and horse racing at the County Fairgrounds in late summer/early fall, and Jazz on the Waterfront and the Stockton RV Sports and Boat Show in mid-fall.

The same civic-mindedness found in these shows and festivals is evident in many of the city's service agencies. Staffed mostly by volunteers, these organizations assist children, senior citizens, recovering alcoholics, the blind, the infirm, and others in need.

Stockton's daily newspaper, the *Record,* runs a Matchmaker program that links up the needs of various nonprofit organizations with individuals and groups that can provide them assistance. This help may come in the form of funding or gifts or the supply of technical equipment. Service organizations seeking assistance include St. Mary's Interfaith Dining Room, the Women's Center, the Easter Seal Society, the Alzheimer's Aid Society, the United Cerebral Palsy Association, and Help the Children.

The city's 150 places of worship represent all major religions and creeds. Some are nearly as old as the city itself. North Pacific's Central United Methodist Church, once located downtown on Miner and El Dorado, dates back to the Gold Rush days of 1849. St. Mary's Catholic Church has remained at San Joaquin and Washington since 1850 on land donated by Charles Weber. Plans for a permanent building began in 1861, but completion of the work took until 1893. The church's spire was restored in 1985, thanks to generous financial support by the public. Other churches more than a hundred years old are Trinity Lutheran and First Congregational, along with Temple Israel.

Two houses of worship of Asian origin bear comment. The Buddhist Temple, completed at Shimizu Drive along Smith's Canal in 1969, makes exquisite use of redwood and Douglas fir, combined with intricately wrought altar designs. The Sikh Temple, founded in 1913, is considered among the first in the United States.

The city provides for the life of the mind, as well. Stockton has a first-rate library system, starting with its handsome central library off the Civic Center on North El Dorado and extending to these branches: Margaret Troke on West Benjamin Holt, Fair Oaks on East Main, and Southeast Stockton on South Airport Way. Other libraries are located in Linden, Manteca, Escalon, Ripon, Tracy, and Thornton.

Among important literary events that occur annually in the city are several symposiums. Local libraries and UOP cooperate to host conferences for writers of mysteries and authors of children's literature. The Stockton Arts Commission and generous patrons have teamed with UOP to sponsor the Marion Jacobs Poetry and Prose Symposium. Speakers at recent symposiums were poet Adrienne Rich and novelist Larry McMurtry. These events are held on the university campus.

Founded in 1851, the University of the Pacific is the oldest chartered

FACING PAGE: Stockton's annual Independence Day extravaganza, the Waterfest, celebrates freedom with the red glare of fireworks reflecting off McLeod Lake, to the delight of thousands of spectators. Photo by Steve Pereira

LEFT: The beautiful Buddhist Temple at Shimizu Drive along Smith's Canal is a peaceful haven, with beautiful woodwork and perfectly manicured grounds. Photo by Steve Pereira

FACING PAGE: Since the late 1800s St. Mary's Catholic Church has invited and inspired worshipers within its walls. Photo by Kerrick James

institution of higher education in California. As it approaches its 140th year, the university—from its verdant main campus in Stockton, to its dental school in San Francisco, to its McGeorge School of Law in Sacramento—has acquired worldwide fame.

The school was started in San Jose by Methodist ministers, and 20 years later it transferred to a new site near Santa Clara. Dr. Tully C. Knoles, who had taken over as president in 1919, directed the final relocation to Stockton in 1924.

Building on the new campus site began modestly. In 1935 the College of the Pacific, as it was then called, restricted its offerings to graduate students and to juniors and seniors in a coordinated effort with public-supported Stockton Junior College. This arrangement lasted until 1951 at the reinstatement of lower division work when Stockton Junior College—now known as San Joaquin Delta College—moved to its own campus on Pacific Avenue. Thus for a long time COP and Delta existed side by side in the city's northwest area.

Over a 30-year span the flamboyant, white-goateed Knoles acquired a reputation as a skillful administrator and colorful character. He liked to ride horseback in parades and show off his prowess with a lasso. He preferred as his mount an enormous white horse that came from the stables of the brother of Emperor Hirohito of Japan.

Under Knoles's successor, the young, innovative Robert E. Burns, who took over as president in 1946, the institution grew rapidly, adding a handful of schools and colleges. President Stanley E. McCaffrey served in the 1970s and early 1980s through a period of continued expansion of campus property, including the old Delta campus, and construction, such as doubling the size of the library. McCaffrey's 16 years in office were interrupted by his one-year term as president of Rotary International. In 1987 Bill L. Atchley, who formerly headed Clemson, became the 22nd president of the university.

Although still maintaining loose ties to the United Methodist Church, the university, from the 1960s on, has been classified as an independent private institution. While fostering research and professional training, the university places its primary emphasis on teaching. Some 5,500 students attend UOP, representing 40 states and about 60 countries, to study more than a hundred majors in liberal arts divisions and in professional programs including law, dentistry, pharmacy, engineering, and education. In a survey conducted by *U.S. News and World Report* in 1988, UOP ranked 22nd nationally among 400 colleges and universities in the comprehensiveness of its various programs. The ranking states: "For a university of Pacific's size, the range of choice is enormous." The faculty totals nearly 400;

University of the Pacific is the state's oldest chartered institution of higher learning. Founded in 1851, UOP has been part of the Stockton community since 1924. Green lawns and green trees evoke the spirit of its Ivy League counterparts in the East. Photo by Kerrick James

Nearly 15,000 students from Stockton and adjacent cities benefit from the vocationally oriented curricula offered by San Joaquin Delta College, the largest public educational institution in Stockton. Photo by Mark E. Gibson

90 percent of them hold the highest degrees in their fields, mostly the Ph.D., and 55 percent are full professors.

By far the largest public educational institution in Stockton is San Joaquin Delta College, a part of the state's community college system. In contrast to the serenely traditional brick and ivy of UOP, Delta's contemporary campus farther north on Pacific Avenue is designed in clusters of stucco buildings that stress unusual angles and planes.

Delta enrolls nearly 15,000 students, many of whom attend classes in outlying communities: Lodi, Galt, and Sutter Creek to the north; Manteca and Escalon to the south; Tracy, Rio Vista, and Isleton to the west; and toward the Mother Lode, Valley Springs, San Andreas, and Jackson. The college offers a two-year academic associate arts degree that is either terminal or preparatory for further university work.

Delta's faculty is large, its fees low, its offerings extensive. For example, the college offers a variety of vocational, technical, and industrial programs. A person who attends Delta can learn to become a brick layer, nurse, carpenter, printer, auto mechanic, computer programmer, tile setter, draftsman, or caterer. Students may choose from subjects as wide ranging as electron microscopy and law enforcement, fire science and food service, physical fitness and horse management. The campus also offers seminars, workshops, and other activities that make it a lively community center.

Students have the option of another private institution on a smaller scale: Humphreys College, located off Benjamin Holt in North Stockton. Now more than 90 years old, this college offers courses, on the quarter system, in general

education, business, and law.

The Stockton Unified School District from pre-kindergarten through 12th grade is large: almost 35,000 students, nearly 50 schools and special programs, almost 1,500 teachers among some 4,000 employees, and a budget of about $130 million. Three public high schools—Edison, Franklin, and Stagg—enroll most students in grades 9 through 12, but five alternative high schools are also available.

LEFT: The Medico-Dental Building on North Sutter, with its streamlined design and 12 stories, remains as beautiful today as it was upon completion in 1928. Photo by Mark E. Gibson

FACING PAGE: Featuring a beautiful red-tiled roof, the six-story Stockton Hotel, built in 1910, is one of the most cherished of Stockton's many historic buildings. Photo by John Elk III

Lincoln Unified School District has 10 schools, including Lincoln High School. Additionally, private schools attract some 5,000 students. Many of these schools are parochial; that is, about a third are Catholic and another third Nazarene, Seventh- Day Adventist, Baptist, Lutheran, and Methodist; the rest are nondenominational. The largest and oldest is St. Mary's High School on North El Dorado, established in the 1870s by the Catholic Church and numbering about 900 students.

The first public schools in Stockton were separate girls' and boys' schools that opened simultaneously in 1853. One of the former public schools—El Dorado Elementary at Harding and Pacific has been declared a historic landmark, joining about 50 other buildings that have been designated as historic landmarks by the Cultural Heritage Board.

Certainly the most eye-catching is the old red-tile-roofed Stockton Hotel, constructed in 1910. Other eye-catchers include the 12-story Medico-Dental Building on North Sutter that was completed in 1928 and the nearby 8-story American Savings Plaza that was finished in 1989. The striking buildings of the Civic Center were built over a lengthy time span: the Memorial Civic Auditorium in 1926, City Hall in 1927, and the Municipal Library in 1964. Having undergone a recent face-lift, the Civic Memorial Auditorium looks ready for another 60 years.

The Newell House, a decorous Victorian on San Joaquin and Magnolia, was built in 1880. When the old Hazelton Library at Market and Hunter was demolished in 1964, its eight Ionic marble columns were moved to UOP, where they now form an attractive colonnade between Knoles Hall and the university library. UOP's well-known buildings have been constructed over a long period: the Conservatory of Music in 1924-1925, Morris Chapel in 1942, Burns Tower in 1963, and the new library in 1987.

If Stocktonians want to witness big-time professional sports, they must drive out of town: for football, to San Francisco to see the 49ers; for baseball, to San

Football fans in Stockton may pass their time watching the UOP football squad butt helmets at the school's spacious, 30,000-seat Amos Alonzo Stagg Memorial Stadium. Photo by Steve Pereira

Francisco to attend a Giants game or to Oakland to see the Athletics; for basketball, to Oakland to cheer the Golden State Warriors, and to Sacramento to root for the Kings. Depending on destination, the drive amounts to less than an hour to less than two hours.

The only professional team in Stockton, the Ports, a baseball farm club of the Milwaukee Brewers, play at 5,000-seat Billy Hebert Field in Oak Park. The Ports compete in a season of two halves in the Class A California League against Fresno, Modesto, Reno, and San Jose in the Northern Division and Bakersfield, Palm Springs, Riverside, San Bernardino, and Visalia in the Southern Division.

Other professional spectator sports include auto racing at the Stockton 99 Speedway on North Wilson Way, horse racing in August at the San Joaquin

County Fair, and occasional boxing, wrestling, and tennis matches, as well as some professional exhibition games.

This Japanese lion is part of the annual Oban Festival held in August. Photo by Steve Pereira

University of the Pacific competes in 12 different men's and women's sports in the NCAA major university division. The football team plays at Amos Alonzo Stagg (formerly Pacific) Memorial Stadium, which seats 30,000. The men's basketball team, also in the Big West Conference, plays in the Spanos Center, as does the NCAA two-time national champion women's volleyball team. The teams play independents and other schools in the Big West Conference.

Delta College also competes in varied men's and women's sports, and Stockton's five high schools compete in the CIF San Joaquin section.

While Stocktonians avidly attend spectator sports, they're even more committed to direct participation in athletics. Mild weather for eight or nine months encourages active involvement in softball, soccer, bowling, tennis, golf, biking, volleyball, racquetball, martial arts, fitness programs, running, and, away from the local scene, skiing in the nearby Sierra. The city has provided some cycling and jogging trails. Softball in particular is enormously popular, with hundreds of teams for children, women, and men.

The Delta waterways afford many recreational benefits. Along with irrigating crops, the Delta has an ecosystem that supports wildlife, in particular migratory birds, and provides a variety of sports and leisure-time activities.

Speedboats, yachts, houseboats, and sailboats ply the thousand miles of waterways. The fishing is great: sturgeon, weighing hundreds of pounds; four varieties of whiskered catfish and of carp; and striped bass from 5 to 25 pounds. Houseboating is popular for stops along low-tide sandy beaches and for gunkholing (overnight anchorages). Nor must one overlook the joys of waterskiing on the Delta. Paddlewheel cruises can be taken on the San Joaquin aboard the *Island Queen,* and varied charters can be taken anywhere. Within the city, three boat launching ramps are available: Louis Park, Buckley Cove off Brookside, and Morelli Ramps under the Crosstown Freeway.

Waterslides have proven popular in Stockton and at Oakwood Lake Resort near Manteca. Camping is available at Mossdale Crossing, Westgate Landing, Dos Rios, and Durham Ferry. The City of Stockton also operates Silver Lake Resort, a family vacation site, during the summer months. The resort is located 100 miles from Stockton at an altitude of 7,200 feet in the Sierra. And Caswell State Park beckons to campers and picnickers in the southern part of the county.

Bounteously endowed as Stockton is with good weather, with numerous outdoor and indoor athletic facilities, and with "water water everywhere," sports and recreation will continue to flourish.

Well worth the drive from Stockton is colorful San Francisco. "The City," as it is known to locals, is unrivaled for its many entertainment, cultural, and sightseeing opportunities. Photo by Kerrick James

Mini Hollywood North

On the basis of the many feature films, TV movies, TV programs, and commercials made in and around Stockton, the area has earned the title of Mini Hollywood North. The unqualified term "Hollywood North" has also been used, but that designation stretches the point.

Stockton got seriously into the movie business in the late 1940s with the filming of *All the King's Men,* which featured a cast of unknowns but went on the following spring to garner three Academy Awards, including Best Picture of the Year for 1949. The film's other Oscar winners were Broderick Crawford as Best Actor in the role of Willie Stark, a Southern demagogue, and Mercedes McCambridge for Best Supporting Actress as Sadie Burke, Willie's wisecracking crony. Oscar nominations also went to Robert Rossen as Best Director and as Screenwriter and to John Ireland as Best Supporting Actor. *All the King's Men* made many uses of Stockton locales. Hundreds of Stocktonians were hired as extras to form crowds for political rallies at the old County Courthouse. The Delta proved a perfect choice as a setting, too, because of its similarity to the Southern Delta depicted in the Robert Penn Warren novel on which the film is based.

In the 1950s five films, all utilizing quite different terrain, were made around Stockton. The Delta waterways served as Chinese rivers for the adventures of *Blood Alley* (1955), with John Wayne and Lauren Bacall, under the direction of William Wellman. More conventional locations were used for *Our Miss Brooks* (1956), with Eve Arden and Gale Gordon. A star-studded cast came to Stockton in 1958 for the shooting of *The Big Country,* with William Wyler as director. Gregory Peck, Jean Simmons, Charlton Heston, Carroll Baker, and Chuck Connors all stayed at the old Stockton Hotel at El Dorado and Weber. Farmland around Farmington was used as sites for the ranches owned by the feuding family patriarchs Burl Ives and Charles Bickford.

Delta farm country substituted for Georgia in *God's Little Acre* (1958), with Robert Ryan and Tina Louise. Similarly the Delta became the bayou in the George Gershwin folk opera *Porgy and Bess* (1959), directed by Otto Preminger and produced by Sam Goldwyn. Sammy Davis, Jr., cavorted around the Delta in the role of Sporting Life for a fish fry sequence. Other denizens of Catfish Row were Dorothy Dandridge, Sidney Poitier, Pearl Bailey, Brock Peters, and Diahann Carroll.

The most well-known movie made in the 1960s in Stockton was *Cool Hand Luke* (1967), which used an oak grove off Davis Road in North Stockton (today's Dentoni Park) as site of a Southern prison farm where the rebel Luke, played by Paul Newman, is sentenced. Some of the locale was sprayed so that it looked like Spanish Moss. Various county roads were used for the convict work scenes, including Highway 4 and a back road to Linden. Director Stuart Rosenberg, Newman, and the large supporting cast of George Kennedy, J.D. Cannon, Strother Martin, Harry Dean Stanton, Anthony Zerbe, and Dennis Hopper were headquartered at the Stockton Inn. The movie also provided a nostalgic return for actress Jo Van Fleet, who was formerly a student at the University of the Pacific.

When Stockton Chamber of Commerce officials calculated the extent to which the local economy benefited from the infusion of Warner Brothers' money for the filming of *Cool Hand Luke,* they decided to turn up their efforts to attract more filmmakers to Stockton and its environs. Their efforts have paid off, though not to the tune of *Cool Hand Luke* (which brought in $625,000 for five weeks of shooting in late 1966). The average feature film made in and around Stockton over recent years pumped between $135,000 and $150,000 into the local economy. Of course, the longer and more complex the film, the greater the return locally.

This area is ideal for filmmaking because of the great variety of its terrain and the mild weather. The Stockton Chamber distributes to film production companies attractive brochures that show off the area's extensive range of locations: open foothill country with a 360-degree unobstructed panorama; river bottoms and swamps that resemble Vietnam or an African jungle; the Delta and lakes, ship channel, and old bridges; farms, vineyards, and plains for outdoor land use; as well as river towns and old railroads.

Also, casting services are available through private firms and through the Employment Development Department, the University of the Pacific and Delta College, and local acting troupes. Hundreds of extras can be summoned in a day, for whatever ethnic mix is required: whether Hispanic, black, Asian, or Anglo.

The moviemaking process is enormously complicated. Stockton has made its locale usable and appealing by providing all necessary services: for airplanes; for trained animals; for bus, car, and truck rentals; for catering services, cleaners, duplicating and printing, emergency medical services, hotels and motels, limousines and locksmiths, bottled water, costumes, cranes and electric generators, props, screening facilities, and security services.

By comparison with the 1970s, the remainder of filming in the sixties was negligible: *Mail Order Bride* (1964), and *Futz* (1969), about a farmer in love with a pig.

The 1970s have turned out to be the richest period for productions so far. With director John Huston, former Stocktonian Leonard Gardner fashioned a tough, hard-hitting screenplay out of his novel *Fat City,* first published in 1969. Stacy Keach and Jeff Bridges played the two mediocre boxers, Billy Tully and Ernie Munger, who are Stockton residents.

Susan Tyrrell's performance as a drunk and the cinematography of Conrad Hall were both distinguished. Huston and Hall made ample use of downtown locations, including the Civic Center and rundown hotels, bars, and cafes. Shooting took place in 1971.

The nearby Peter Ospital ranch served as setting for *Oklahoma Crude* (1973), directed by Stanley Kramer, with Faye Dunaway as a stubborn oil well owner and George C. Scott as a buffoon who helps her to fight off a greedy oil baron, played by Jack Palance.

Some scenes of *American Graffiti* (1973) took place in southern San Joaquin County, but most were shot in Modesto (director George Lucas' hometown) and in Petaluma. The movie, about high school grads in a 1962 small town, starred Richard Dreyfuss, Ron Howard, Charles Martin Smith, Cindy Williams, and Harrison Ford. Its sequel, *More American Graffiti* (1979), also filmed nearby, with a half-dozen of the original cast but sans Dreyfuss and Ford, turned out as a pale imitation of the original.

Director Hal Ashby and cinematographer Haskell Wexler combined forces to make an affective *Bound for Glory* (1976), in which David Carradine played Woody Guthrie. The movie follows the singer-songwriter's life and career during the Depression. Rural locales in San Joaquin County were used for important scenes of *Who'll Stop the Rain* (1978), with Nick Nolte, Tuesday Weld, and Michael Moriarty. The movie concerns the consequences of smuggling drugs to California from Vietnam. Four other films shot locally in the 1970s were *The Moonshine War* (1970), a comedy-drama set in the prohibition era, with Alan Alda and Richard Widmark; *Dirty Mary, Crazy Larry* (1974), featuring Peter Fonda, Susan George, and Adam Roarke as three young people on the lam after a robbery; *Purple Haze* (1978), with Peter Nelson and Chuck McQuary as alienated youth in the summer of 1968; and *Alex and the Gyspy* (1976), starring Jack Lemmon, Genevieve Bujold, and James Woods, and using more than a hundred parishioners of Stockton's St. Basil Greek Orthodox Church as extras. This romance between a bailbondsman and a gypsy was shot in and around Sonora and elsewhere in the Mother Lode.

The 1980s began with *Coast to Coast,* a road comedy about a trucker (Robert Blake) and a woman on the run (Dyan Cannon). Some of the film was shot at Jim Orvis' Farmington ranch (also used in *The Big Country*). One scene brought gales of laughter from cast, crew, and onlookers: a careening truck tips, causing its cargo of chickens to flee in all directions over city streets. The mall scenes in *Valley Girl* (1983), a romance between a punker (Nicholas Cage) and a suburban girl (Deborah Foreman), were shot in the Weberstown Mall, under the direction of Martha Coolidge.

Stockton continues to remain active in recruiting filmmakers to the area. For example, in 1987 the Stockton Chamber of Commerce attracted a group of Hollywood production coordinators and location managers for a two-day FAM (familiarization) tour. Led by Dave Smith, the Stockton film commissioner, the group toured the Ospital ranch and the Orvis ranch, and the areas of Jenny Lind, Farmington, Escalon, and Ripon. In the later afternoon and evening they cruised the Delta and returned to Stockton's Waterfront area. On the second day, again guided by Smith, they toured Lodi, Woodbridge, Thornton, Walnut Grove, Locke, and Isleton. Then later they toured the University of the Pacific campus, Stockton residential areas, and Caswell State Park. The group left for its return to Los Angeles much impressed with the tremendous variety of locations available in the Stockton vicinity.

One particular locale has been popular with producers of movies about college life: the campus of the University of the Pacific. Admired for the beauty of its grounds and buildings, UOP gives the appearance of Eastern halls of ivy. The trend toward use of the campus for movies began in 1959 when Bing Crosby was cast in the role of a widower who goes back to college. Under the direction of Blake Edwards, Crosby teamed with Tuesday Weld and Fabian in the comedy released as *High Time* in 1960.

Rioting on university campuses in the sixties became the subject of two films released in 1970. The first, *RPM* (for revolutions per minute), starred Anthony Quinn as a liberal professor who takes over the job of university president and opposes campus radicals. The picture, also featuring Ann-Margret and directed by Stanley Kramer, made prominent use of the grounds around Knoles Hall. An equally undistinguished film about the student takeover of buildings at Columbia University, *The Strawberry Statement,* with Bruce Davison and Kim Darby, primarily used Stockton City Hall and the Civic Center for its locales. Many otherwise peaceable UOP students hired as extras had a grand time as rioters.

A Disney comedy, *The World's Greatest Athlete* (1973), starring John Amos as a coach and Jan-Michael Vincent as a super-athlete, was shot on the UOP campus and at the old Delta college track. Area residents remember vividly the huge Bengal tiger parading around the university's front entrance as a team mascot in one scene.

The UOP campus was put to quite different use in *Dreamscape* (1984), with Dennis Quaid, Kate Capshaw, and Max von Sydow. With its emphasis on research into scary dreams, the usually serene ivy-covered Knoles Hall was transformed into an ominous and forbidding research center. Several UOP campus locations were used to duplicate an Eastern college during seasonal changes in *The Sure Thing* (1985), directed by Rob Reiner and featuring John Cusack, Daphne Zuniga, and bicycle-riding professor Arlen J. Hansen. The picture illustrates perfectly the magical transformation possible in film. For one thing, fake snow was spread on green grass to create the impression of winter. For another, UOP's Khoury Hall, an engineering building containing offices, classrooms, and labs, serves as the entrance into the movie college's indoor swimming pool. A similar transformation occurred in Steven Spielberg's *Raiders of the Lost Ark* (1981). When archeologist-explorer Indiana Jones (Harrison Ford) returns from his hair-raising exploits to lecture in a quiet classroom, the exterior of UOP's then unrenovated Conservatory of Music is shown as the classroom building.

Such exterior shots take up only a few seconds of film time. Occasionally local terrain is used only for a snippet of a film. For instance, in the movie *Birdy* (1984), directed by Alan Parker and starring Matthew Modine and Nicolas Cage, Vietnam was re-created out of rugged southern San Joaquin County terrain for one brief, explosive war scene.

Some films fail to achieve national release and never fulfill their expectations. *Good Luck, Miss Wyckoff* (retitled *The Sin*) seemed to have everything going for it when made here in 1978. Based on the only novel by playwright William Inge, the movie featured a veteran cast of Anne Heywood, Earl Holliman, Robert Vaughn, Carolyn Jones, and Dorothy Malone, and scores of local extras. The picture, which is about the consequences of a teacher's repressed sexuality, shot for 35 days in a variety of Stockton locations such as the old El Dorado School, the Lodi Women's Club, and several residential areas of Central Stockton. The movie crashed before it could take off.

So, too, did the movie *Rampage* that had an elaborate premiere at the Stockton Royal Theater in January 1988. Directed by William Friedkin and featuring Michael Biehn, Deborah Van Valkenburg, and Alex McArthur, *Rampage* was supposed to be an intense examination of the criminal justice system, but instead it turned into a mad-slasher flick. The production company found itself in financial limbo, and the movie has not been released for national audiences. Too bad, because they would have got a good look at numerous Stockton locations, including homes on Bristol Avenue, a service station on south California, Superior Court in the County Courthouse, the El Dorado Street overpass, the Waterfront area, and Mossdale Bridge. That movie used dozens of Stockton extras, among them a police officer, a district attorney, and a Catholic priest.

Two other films shot recently in Stockton are *An American Murder* (1987), which has not achieved wide release, and *Valentino Returns* (1985), which was finally released in summer 1989. The latter, starring Frederic Forrest, Veronica Cartwright, and Barry Tubb, was filmed from a screenplay by Leonard Gardner.

Some plans for movies don't materialize. For example, the makers of *Tai-pan* (1986), based on James Clavell's sweeping novel, intended to use an island in the Delta for much of the shooting, but the deal fell through. (The movie turned out to be a dud.)

Of the many television films shot here, among the more celebrated was *Friendly Fire,* made in the summer of 1978, with Carol Burnett in her first dramatic role, Ned Beatty, and then-newcomer Timothy Hutton. Another was *Raid on Entebbe,* featuring Peter Finch and Charles Bronson, which was made in November 1976, only four months after the actual event in Africa. Director Irvin Kershner and a sizable cast and crew took over the Stockton Municipal Airport and its runways. Air traffic was disrupted for a time, diverting a plane or two scheduled to land in Stockton on to Sacramento. The University of the Pacific campus, A.A. Stagg Memorial football stadium, the Stockton Country Club, and other local sites were used for a TV movie shown in late 1988; *Glory Days* featured Robert Conrad in the role of a retired 53-year-old tire dealer who decides to attend his hometown university and play football.

Many episodes of television programs were shot locally: among them "Little House on the Prairie," "The Big Valley," "Happy Days," and "Then Came Bronson." One frustration that Stockton has had to face is losing TV series after the pilots had been filmed here. According to Vince Perrin, executive director of the Stockton Arts Commission, the pilots to "The Man Hunter," "Kin Folks," "B.J. and the Bear," and "Then Came Bronson" were all shot around Stockton, but then moved back to Southern California and elsewhere for prolonged shooting. As Dave Smith of the Chamber of Commerce comments, "We've had plenty of pilots, but no flights."

Smith and Perrin concur that the loss is more keenly felt when programs become long-running hits, such as "Little House on the Prairie" and "Happy Days," both pilots of which were made here, the latter first titled "Senior Year." And, as with the loss of an occasional movie such as *Tai-pan,* a TV mini-series may be lost. Stockton came close to bagging *The Thorn Birds,* but the producers chose to use Southern California as their substitute for Australia.

In recent years numerous television commercials have been shot locally. The variety of terrain, good weather, reasonable costs, and availability of actors and services have been factors in attracting makers of commercials.

All in all, Stockton's track record in film and TV over the years has been impressive, and the area continues to draw filmmakers. Certainly enough to retain the title Mini Hollywood North.

San Joaquin County is home to cities Manteca and Tracy, as well as Stockton, and is known for its farmland and waterways, such as the Mokelumne River shown here. Photo by Kerrick James

Chapter **5**

Good Neighbors

The Greek letter Delta forms a triangle. It is appropriate that in country known as the Delta, Stockton should be at the heart of San Joaquin County and in the center of a triangle formed by three moderate-sized cities: Lodi, Manteca, and Tracy.

Before we get acquainted with these good neighbors, and other smaller ones, we need to examine the county itself. (San Joaquin, by the way, is Spanish for Saint Joachim.) San Joaquin County is bounded on the north by Sacramento County, on the south by Stanislaus County, on the west by Alameda and Contra Costa counties, and on the east by Amador and Calaveras counties. Aside from the start of the Sierra foothills to the east and lower portions of the Diablo range to the southwest, the entire region consists of rich, flat farmland that

Potato Slough and Disappointment Slough are just a few of the tracts and Sloughs that are connected by the San Joaquin County waterways. Photo by Kerrick James

benefits from a long growing season. The farmland covers nearly 800,000 acres, roughly one-twelfth of the Central Valley's 11 million acres that stretch from north of Sacramento to south of Bakersfield.

Of the 58 counties in California, San Joaquin ranks as the 15th largest. It covers almost 1,500 square miles, and its population is headed toward the half-million mark. About half of its residents live in Stockton, suburban Morada, and unincorporated areas of Stockton as socioeconomically diverse as Garden Acres, Lincoln Village, and Riviera Cliffs. The other half lives in the triumverate of Lodi-Manteca-Tracy, in two smaller cities, Ripon and Escalon, and in a couple dozen other unincorporated areas around the county. In summer 1989 balloting citizens of Lathrop voted for incorporation. As a result, Lathrop, which is located directly south of Stockton, became San Joaquin County's seventh city.

Let's survey these neighbors by starting to the north and working clockwise. The largest city is Lodi, with a population of about 50,000. Smaller communities around it include Acampo, Woodbridge, Forest Lake (or Collierville), and Henderson Village.

To the northeast, the largest town is Lockeford, at about 2,000 inhabitants.

Other unincorporated communities around it include Clements, Victor, and Waterloo. To the east lie four other small farming communities: Linden, Peters, Bellota, and Farmington.

Explosive growth has occurred to the southeast, particularly in Manteca, where the population is now nearly 40,000. Nearby Ripon and Escalon have reached populations of 7,000 and 4,000, respectively. Other unincorporated areas in the vicinity include Turner, Five Corners, Collegeville, and Sims.

A popular area in the southeast that borders the Stanislaus River is Caswell Memorial State Park, the only state park in San Joaquin County. Filled with valley oak, its 258 acres also contain campgrounds, trails, and a bathing beach. The Durham Ferry Recreation area, a county-operated neighbor to the west along the San Joaquin River, is less frequented than Caswell, mostly because of its lack of shade trees.

In addition to Lathrop, to the south of Stockton lie French Camp, San Joaquin River Club, and Vernalis. At last count, as a newly incorporated city, Lathrop numbers 6,000 inhabitants.

To the southwest, another city that has experienced substantial growth in the last few decades is Tracy, now at a population of 30,000. Banta, Mossdale, Carbona, and Bethany are unincorporated settlements around Tracy. To the northwest lie two other unincorporated communities: Thornton and Terminous.

Anyone traveling the area to the west of Stockton—whether due west, southwest, or northwest—will be struck by the Delta land's wondrous topography. The area consists of a baker's dozen of tremendously productive islands, all richly planted with a variety of crops: King, Empire, Venice, Mandeville, Medford, Mildred, McDonald, Bacon, Victoria, Union, Roberts, Staten, and Bouldin. In addition, the Delta contains 11 tracts, not quite islands, that are well irrigated and equally productive: New Hope, Rindge, Shin-Kee, Shima, Wright, Brack, Lower Jones, Upper Jones, Terminous, Atlas, and Bishop. Rough and Ready Island, at the western edge of Stockton bordering the channel, serves as home to the large, long-established U.S. Naval Communication Station.

A fantastic water network nourishes the entire region. Interlacing dozens of sloughs, including major ones like Potato Slough, Fourteen Mile Slough, and Disappointment Slough, are forks of the Mokelumne River and the San Joaquin River, the Calaveras River and its diverting canal, Smith's Canal, and Duck Creek, not to mention a series of man-made lakes: Grupe, North, Lincoln, Meadow, Quail, and Venezia. San Joaquin County is also fortunate to have an abundance of water from underground sources and from reservoirs in high terrain east of Stockton—New Hogan, New Melones, and others—to supply homes, farms, and industries.

Now to "shake hands" with a few neighbors. First is Lodi, located 13 miles to the north, between highways 5 and 99 and joined by 12. Founded in 1869 and originally called Mokelumne Station, it was incorporated in 1906. Three stories have circulated about the source for the name Lodi: (1) a prominent race horse of the 1860s, (2) an agricultural area in Italy and scene of a battle in the Napoleonic Wars, and (3) the town of Lodi, Illinois, from which some settlers came. The last source seems most likely.

Lodi's growth remained steady but low at 2 percent annually over a number of decades. Since 1981, however, the city has undergone a 4 percent growth rate.

Lodi has acquired a reputation as a quiet, clean, orderly, conservative city. Its streets are wide and tree shaded, its houses and yards well tended. The Mokelumne River twists through the northern part, forming at its center Lodi Lake, an attractive recreation area.

Vineyards surround Lodi. The grapes come in many varieties, in appealing hues of green, red, purple, and nearly black. The Flame Tokay, first planted in the 1970s, is probably the most well known. Nearly all Tokay grapes grown in the world come from a 10-mile radius around Lodi. In fact, Lodi ships almost one million pounds of Tokay grapes annually. Nine wineries conduct business within the immediate area.

Nearly a hundred manufacturing plants operate in and around Lodi. The city has an extremely large school district of some 22,000 students. In fact, the

Lodi's landmark arch serves as a gateway to a city known for a quiet and orderly life-style. Photo by Kerrick James

Paradise Point Marina serves as a departure point for boaters in San Joaquin County. Photo by Kerrick James

school district prevails as Lodi's major employer (with 2,000 employees), followed by General Mills (in a plant occupying close to 100 acres) and Pacific Coast Producers.

If the rock group Credence Clearwater Revival gently chided Lodi back in the sixties with its song about being "stuck in Lodi," many city residents would reply that it's a pretty nicc place to be stuck.

Manteca dominates the southeast corner of the Delta triumverate. Homesteaded by Joshua Cowell and for a time called Cowell Station, the village was renamed Manteca in 1897 and incorporated in 1918. The name purportedly derived from a misspelling on railroad tickets, but the story seems apocryphal; most likely the name resulted from corruption of a Spanish word.

For decades Manteca remained a small town; in 1970 its population stood at just under 14,000. Then the population explosion occurred: in 20 years it tripled in size. The latest land-use diagram for Manteca shows a redoubling in size in all directions in the not-too-distant future. Such growth is amazing when one considers that in 1910 it was a tiny farming community of less than 100.

However, rate of growth remains a subject of controversy in Manteca. By a narrow majority in a November 1988 ballot initiative, voters defeated a proposal for an annual cap of 2 percent, thus accepting an in-place growth rate of 3.9 percent.

Some estimates place Manteca's commuting labor force as higher than 40 percent; among these are several thousand who travel back and forth between their residential subdivisions and thc Bay Area. Although Manteca has been dubbed a bedroom community, it has recently become home base for a couple dozen manufacturing plants specializing in glass, chemicals, auto supplies, fertilizers, seeds, and electronic products. Sugar beets grown in surrounding areas are shipped to Manteca for processing. Spreckels Sugar Refinery—now Spreckels-Amstar—has been operating intermittently in the city since World War I.

Wineries such as Franzia and Delicato employ a substantial work force. But by far the largest employer is the Sharpe Army Depot in Lathrop, where some 1,500 civilians are on the government payroll.

As the Sharpe Depot draws Mantecans to Lathrop, so does the newly planned 540-acre Kearny Industrial Park which is on the Lathrop side of the borderline between the two neighbors. Also, privately owned Oakwood Lake Resort has become a major water sports attraction nearby.

For a long while Tracy led a dual existence as an agricultural center and as "Railroad City." The latter designation recalls Tracy's founding in 1878 as an extension of a Southern Pacific rail line. Relocation of an adjoining town called Ellis

Spreckels Sugar Refinery, Known as Spreckels-Amstar, is a large employer in Manteca. Raw sugar is stockpiled in the foreground. Photo by Kerrick James

helped to boost the city's growth. Named after Lathrop J. Tracy, an Ohio merchant who never set foot on its soil, Tracy continued as a railroad stop for many years.

Surrounded as Tracy was by potentially fertile farmland, irrigation played a major part in the city's development, particularly by the formation in 1915 of the West Side Irrigation District. Areas like Tracy blossomed when irrigation water allowed farmers to shift from limited dry farming to varied crop planting. In place of grains came beets, fruit trees, alfalfa, lima beans, and an assortment of market crops, such as asparagus, tomatoes, carrots, and lettuce.

Other highlights of Tracy's history, in brief, include: incorporation in 1910; installation of the Holly Sugar plant in 1917; the building of the Tracy Inn in 1927; and the opening of the H.J. Heinz plant in 1946. Construction began on the Deuel Vocational Institution in 1949; this prison, completed in 1953 to accommodate 1,200 inmates, has now swollen to nearly three times that size. The Tracy Defense Depot, started in World War II, has continued to expand and now employs 1,600 civilians.

Tracyites consider their greatest accomplishment to have been statewide water projects. As part of the Central Valley Project, the huge Tracy Pumping Plant, dedicated in 1951, raises water 200 feet from the Sacramento River into the Delta-Mendota Canal for use by the lower San Joaquin Valley. Six 22,500-horsepower motors drive the massive pumps that are capable of outputting 3 million gallons of water per day. This feat is ranked with another key water project connected to multipurpose reclamation: completion in 1967 of the Delta Pumping Plant that carries surplus Northern California water by canal and pipeline some 440 miles to Southern California.

As the 1990s beckon, Tracy continues to move into another phase of development, this time as a bedroom community for the Bay Area. The city's growth is evident in these population figures: 2,500 in 1920; 8,500 in 1950; and 13,500 in 1965. With more than 30,000 residents today, Tracy's population has more than doubled in 20-plus years. Tracy encouraged this growth by offering affordable houses and good-sized lots to prospective home buyers. The city is also known for its strong school system and excellent health facilities.

The attractive little town of Ripon has doubled in size in the last decade. Originally called Stanislaus, it was renamed after Ripon, Wisconsin, the birthplace of the community's founder, A.B. Cook. Like so many other cities in the county it began as a railroad town and center of dry farming, but its character changed with the advent of irrigation and the concomitant decline of railway business.

Ripon has attracted such big industries as Nestlé (makers of Nescafe and Nestea), the Simpson Paper Company (producers of varied paper products), and Guntert and Zimmerman (manufacturers of steel and heavy construction equipment). However, it is most noted for its surrounding grape vineyards and almond orchards. In fact, Ripon proudly labels itself "The Almond Capital of the World."

Two footnotes: Ripon has a sizable population of Swiss descent, and the town smells good—from the aromas, mostly coffee, drifting from the Nestlé's plant and when, over a fortnight, almond trees blossom everywhere.

The incorporation of Ripon in 1945 seems recent, yet its neighbor Escalon followed even later, incorporating in 1957.

Escalon has been content to live up to its name as "stepping stone" (from the Spanish) rather than attempt to be a boulder. This community doesn't mind staying within the population range of 4,000, which is double its size at incorporation. While it encourages businesses to come in, so far Escalon has discouraged excess population. To ensure slow growth, the city has recently allowed only 75 housing permits per year. Agriculture (mainly fruits, nuts, and vegetables) provides its principal means of livelihood, although within the city itself Hogan Steel Manufacturing is the major employer.

ABOVE AND BELOW: *One of the many area wineries, the Delicato Winery is open for visiting. Photos by Kerrick James*

As might be expected, some places within the county derive their names from their settlers, or their function. For example, Lockeford was originally Locke's Ford, after Dr. Dean Jewett Locke, an enterprising physician from Boston who came across the country in 1849. He built and maintained a ford across the Mokelumne River. Similarly, Woodbridge began as (Jeremiah H.) Woods' Bridge and until 1862 was known as Woods' Ferry. Thornton, originally called New Hope, is named after its early Scottish settler Arthur Thornton.

Lathrop was named after Leland Stanford's wife Jane, whose maiden name was Lathrop, and after Stanford's brother-in-law Charles Lathrop. The town itself resulted from a snub by the City of Stockton, which refused to grant right-of-way for the Central Pacific Railroad. The angry Stanford, a powerful politician and railroad czar, moved the Central Pacific's route to

San Joaquin County benefits from many engineering achievements, such as the California Aqueduct and power-generating windmills. Photo by Kerrick James

Lathrop, then known as Wilson's Station, and swore that Lathrop would thrive and Stockton would dwindle.

Things didn't turn out as Stanford had planned. However, Lathrop has grown into a busy little city. It boasts the huge Sharpe Army Depot, established early in World War II and modernized often since, a Simplot fertilizer and chemical plant, and a Libby-Owens glass plant.

Some of these surrounding towns trumpet their virtues in annual celebrations: in February the Ripon Almond Blossom Festival (held since 1963); in April the Clements Stampede, a lively small rodeo; in May the Linden Cherry Harvest Festival; in August the Tracy Bean Festival; in September a grape stomp at Manteca and the largest of the events, the Lodi Grape Festival; and in late September or early October the Manteca Pumpkin Fair.

A few communities in the county have faded into oblivion, for varied reasons. Nature disposed of Mokelumne City, about three miles north of Thornton on the south bank of the Mokelumne—the floods of 1862 wiped the community out, under eight feet of water. San Joaquin City, a bustling river town established in 1849 (at Kasson Road one-half mile south of Airport Way), disappeared early in the next century because of shifts in commerce and transportation, not to mention the altered course of the San Joaquin River.

A third disappearance, and the most unusual, involved Carnegie, developed in a canyon on the Corral Hollow Road nine miles southwest of Tracy. Around the turn of the century, the Tesla Mine produced up to a thousand tons of coal a day. The plant of the Carnegie Brick and Pottery Company had 45 kilns, 13 tall smokestacks, and produced, at its height, 80,000 bricks a day. The Alameda and San Joaquin Railroad provided freight service on a regular basis. The town, boasting 1,200 residents, contained a post office and company store, a hotel and saloon, large bunkhouses, and several hundred single-family homes.

Growth in Tracy, both in employment and new construction, is a result of a prosperous agriculture industry. Photo by Kerrick James

Now nothing remains of this once-thriving community. Nothing. However, in recent years the land itself has become the site of the Carnegie State Vehicular Recreation area where drivers race their motorcycles and offroad vehicles up and down its steep trails. For a time it appeared that a new 6,000-acre community—to be called Carnegie New Town—might develop there in the mid-1990s, but the project evaporated, just as the old town did. It may well reappear in time.

Who could have foretold that these old towns would vanish? By the same token, who can predict with any certainty what the future holds for San Joaquin County, particularly Stockton? Nevertheless, some projections into the next century can be attempted.

Recreational boaters have a paradise in San Joaquin County's extensive waterways, where waters are calm enough for houseboating or waterskiing. Photo by Kerrick James

Day Trips and Overnighters

While Stockton is a pleasing place to call home, it also happens to be in the middle of an enticing circle of attractions, all within a radius of 130 miles. The radius of that circle sweeps over a huge treasure chest, filled with natural and man-made wonders and enjoyable tourist activities. Hop in the car and soon you're there: the average short drive takes an hour; the average lengthier driving time is 2½ hours.

Thus, aside from the many reasons cited by Stocktonians for liking the city they live in, they also relish its centrality of location. It's close to many places they want to visit. And the places are all so different: from ocean shore to mountain top to winding river; from urban skyscraper to children's theme park to old Gold Rush town to primitive wilderness.

In some instances, where the drive is lengthier and much awaits to see and do—like a trip to Monterey or Yosemite—you might prefer to stay overnight. In that case, always try to make your reservations in advance, whether for lodging or camping.

Any number of opportunities present themselves for travel in **The Delta,** which is interlaced by four rivers (the San Joaquin, Mokelumne, Sacramento, and Calaveras) and by many sloughs. Remember that much of the driving takes place on roads atop banked levees that twist along rivers and sloughs, so be cautious.

One sample short day trip from Stockton into the Delta would take you on Highway 12 west to *Terminous,* then north along the Sacramento River through *Isleton,* a small river town where rests the old-time dredge *Neptune.* Next, pass through *Walnut Grove,* home of the two Walnut Grove TV towers, the tallest structures in the U.S. Then on to the dwindling, weathered community of *Locke,* where 1,500 Chinese once lived. Around a bend and along Steamboat Slough, you come upon a palatial estate, the *Grand Island Mansion,* built in 1917 and now popularly used for parties and various social functions. The trip is abetted by two ferry boat crossings at Howard's Landing and Ryer Island. The last stop before returning to Stockton comes at *Rio Vista,* a sizable river town at the western end of the Rio Vista Bridge that spans the broad Sacramento. A memorial has been placed on the river bank in Rio Vista to commemorate the celebrated three-week period in the fall of 1984 when Humphrey, the humpback whale, cavorted in the river and adjoining sloughs before returning to the open sea.

About an hour and a half away from Stockton to the northwest is **Marine World Africa USA** in Vallejo. An education center, zoo, circus, and safari all wrapped up into one, this multifaceted park features whales, dolphins, and seals performing in water shows, and lions, tigers, apes, giraffes, and exotic birds in their natural habitat. The park holds 1,000 animals in all. Visitors can ride elephants, watch water skiing acrobatics, and witness remarkable trained-animal acts.

Great America lies to the southwest in Santa Clara, a bit more than an hour's drive from Stockton. Spread over 100 acres, this largest amusement park in Northern California is divided into five theme areas: Hometown Square, Yankee Harbor, New Orleans Place, Yukon Territory, and County Fair. Great America offers enough rides, films, concerts, and shows to keep young and old entertained through a day.

The **Napa and Sonoma Wine Country,** about an hour and a half from Stockton, makes for an alluring trip. One popular route begins at Napa and extends upward into the *Napa Valley,* through Yountsville, St. Helena, and Calistoga. Another comes south from Healdsburg and takes in Santa Rosa, Glen Ellen, and Sonoma in the *Sonoma Valley.* More than 200 wineries offer tours and wine tasting. The drive in either valley is pleasurable as you wend along rolling green hills, neatly planted vineyards, and impressive estates. Other wine tasting tours can be taken through wineries in the Great Valley in the Sierra foothills. Of course, every wine-tasting trip is safest when the driver chooses to be a non-drinker.

Next, swing north to **Sacramento,** only 50 minutes from central Stockton, to the steps of the *State Capitol.* Modeled after our nation's capitol in Washington, D.C., this imposing building of Roman Corinthian design contains a dome 210 feet high. When renovation was completed after six years in 1981 at a cost of $68 million, the original beauty of the interior had been restored: intricate tile floors, sweeping staircases, shimmering chandeliers, and large murals. The building houses historical memorabilia and displays from all of the state's counties. The grounds of Capitol Park cover 40 acres and contain many different trees and shrubs.

Old Town, a duplication of Sacramento of the mid-1800s, is also conveniently located downtown right off the freeway on 27 acres along the Sacramento River. Its hundred buildings, adjoined by wooden sidewalks, include restaurants, businesses, and boutiques. Old Town also contains the *California State Historical Railroad Museum,* displaying almost two dozen beautifully restored railroad cars and locomotives, including a giant Southern Pacific steam locomotive that weighs over 500 tons. A tuneful time to visit Old Town is over the Memorial Day weekend, when more than a hundred Dixieland Jazz bands gather to entertain—the event has become the biggest jazz festival in the world.

The *Sacramento Zoo* provides entertainment for the entire family. The zoo, in William Land Park, endeavors to re-create natural settings for its 700 animals. Young children have joyous fun at its neighboring Fairytale Town and playground.

Other Sacramento attractions include *Sutter's Fort* and adjoining *State Indian Museum; Cal Expo,* the site of the state fair that is held for almost three weeks every late summer; the *Crocker Art Museum,* the oldest public art museum in the West; and the *Sacramento and American rivers* for swimming, boating, and fishing.

If you enjoy mouth-watering apple pie, sauces, and other kinds of apple treats, spend an autumn day at *Apple Hill* east of Placerville off Highway 50. Apples of the region are produced by about 50 participating growers.

To the south off Highway 88 look for *Indian Grinding Rock State Park,* dedicated to Indian culture. And also worth seeing in the vicinity in early spring is *Daffodil Hill,* not far from the Gold Rush town of Volcano. Visitors can hike and have picnics around its six acres of blooming yellow flowers.

East of Stockton, within an hour-and-a-half drive, a series of excellent attractions beckon: the dozen **Gold Rush Towns** that lie in Stanislaus, Calaveras, Amador, and Tuolumne counties.

Routes toward them vary. One way starts to the south past Oakdale at *Knight's Ferry,* which dates to the first ferry crossing of the Stanislaus River in the Gold Rush days. The town also contains a covered bridge more than a block long. The next stop is *Jamestown,* where gold mining still goes on. Then a short three-mile climb leads to *Sonora,* the biggest town the Gold Rush created. The architecture of this thriving community blends adobe structures, stately frame Victorians, and modern styles.

Nearby *Columbia State Historical Park* has been authentically reconstructed so that the town of Columbia looks the way it did during the Gold Rush. Even the clerks wear historical costumes. Visitors can pan for gold and ride in a stagecoach. No cars are permitted in the town itself.

To the north of Columbia lies historic *Angel's Camp,* which retains much of the flavor of its early days when Mark Twain observed it. In fact, if you don't mind heavy traffic and throngs of visitors, bring your frog along to the *Calaveras Frog Jumping Contest* in May in Angel's Camp.

Farther up the highway is colorful *Murphy's.* The Murphy's Hotel has been operating continuously since before the Civil War when visitors first began touring the groves at *Calaveras Big Trees.* The hiking trails of Big Trees State Park (off Highway 4) wind through magnificent stands of redwoods, sugar pine, cedar, and ponderosa pine. Also, underground attractions for tourists, *Mercer Caverns* and *Moaning Caves,* are both near Murphy's. And not to be missed farther up on Highway 4 are meadowy *Bear Valley* and crystal-clear *Lake Alpine.*

These visits have by now exhausted a day or two. So, armed with a map and new plans, continue again the discovery of the golden chain, this time taking in east-west Highways 26 and 88 and short jaunts on 124, 12, and 49. *Jackson* remains a bustling town. Especially entertaining are the sing-alongs at the old National Hotel saloon. Nearby are the *Kennedy Mine Tailing Wheels* from the early part of the twentieth century. The huge wheels carried thousands of tons of tailings over a ridge from a stamping mill. Other Gold Rush towns along 49 include *Amador City, Sutter Creek,* and *Mokelumne Hill.* A prospering community farther south is San Andreas, where the famous stagecoach robber Black Bart was once jailed.

Visits to these dozen towns of the Mother Lode will surely give the visitor a feeling of what life was like back in the Gold Rush years. If more avid pursuit is desired, drive farther north and east of Sacramento to the four counties of El Dorado, Placer, Nevada, and Sierra. Visit the *Marshall Gold Discovery State Park* that includes a replica of Sutter's Mill and part of the community of Coloma. Larger towns in the vicinity that have grown from days of old include Placerville, Grass Valley, and Auburn.

Back on Highway 88 families can head up into the High Sierra to stay at the *Silver Lake Resort,* operated by the City of Stockton, Department of Parks and Recreation. The resort provides camping facilities, tents and cabins, food service, nature study, swimming, hiking, arts and crafts, and various sports activities.

Only a couple of hours away from Stockton to the northeast is **Lake Tahoe,** bearing now, along with reflections of tall pines, the shadows of high-rise casino hotels. In all, Tahoe—as it's popularly called—boasts 16,000 hotel and motel rooms. The major growth has occurred at the south and north ends. Places of great beauty still abound once you get away from the hamburger stands and the neon signs and the exhaust smoke. The lake itself, the largest Alpine lake in North America, is 12 miles wide and 22 miles long, with marinas and beaches scattered along its shoreline. Also, in surrounding woods Tahoe contains two dozen campgrounds. Winter sports are popular at Tahoe as well.

High Sierra ski areas include Squaw Valley, site of the 1960 Winter Olympic Games, with 26 lifts; Heavenly Valley, also with 26 lifts; Alpine Meadows, 13 lifts; Northstar, 11 lifts; Kirkwood, 10 lifts; Sugar Bowl, 9 lifts; Mount Reba/Bear Valley, 9 lifts; and a dozen more. Also, trails for cross-country skiing, routes for snowmobiling, and hills for sleds and toboggans can be found.

Besides Lake Tahoe, other large bodies of water within the circle of treasures around Stockton are *Folsom Dam,* just east of Sacramento; *Oroville Dam* to the north; *Berryessa* to the northwest; and closer to home to the east, *Lake Comanche* and *Hogan Reservoir.*

For hikers, backpackers, and inveterate fishermen, a few **Wilderness Areas** remain untouched. You need to get a permit from a local branch of the U.S. Forest Service before you set out on an overnighter. Two recommended wilderness areas within two to three hours driving distance of Stockton are the *Desolation Valley Wild Area,* consisting of 100 square miles just west of Lake Tahoe along Highway 50 on Emerald Bay Road, and the *Emigrant Basin Wild Area* north of Yosemite off Highway 108. Granite walled mountains, forested valleys, muscular rivers, and streams await the hardy nature lover.

The High Sierra consists of magnificent mountain ranges more than a mile high and 400 miles long and contains, along with eight national forests and a thousand lakes, three major national parks.

Yosemite, one of the oldest national parks in the U.S., remains one of the greatest and certainly among the most popular. Two routes can be taken from Stockton, both beginning on Highway 99 south: the shorter but somewhat more demanding back way route on Highway 120, and the less taxing but longer way through Merced, then on to Highway 140. The drives take about 2½ hours.

In a canyon carved eons ago by a glacier lies *Yosemite Valley,* surrounded by huge granite cliffs washed here and there by waterfalls. The names bespeak romance: *El Capitan, Bridal Veil Falls, Cathedral Rocks, Vernal Falls, Sentinel Rock,* and *Three Brothers.* If you stay just on the valley floor, you miss much. The park, after all, covers 1,200 square miles and contains 700 miles of hiking trails and 30 miles of bridle trails. At full runoff the falls are spectacular, such as Yosemite Falls, almost 2,700 feet down, the height of 16 Niagaras.

A range of lodging is available, from fancy hotels to spartan canvas-covered cabins to outdoor camping, but be sure always to make reservations in advance and, if arriving late, to confirm them earlier. Remember, too, that Tioga Road east of Crane Flat is closed to vehicles in the winter. If you can get into the back country where crowds thin out, you have a chance to appreciate even more the grandeur of Yosemite.

The two other great national parks of the Sierra, *Sequoia* and *Kings Canyon,* adjoin one another farther south from Yosemite. However, they exceed in distance the 130-mile limit from Stockton. Within reach, though, and worth visiting is **Fresno** (eighth in the state in population), which is due west of Sequoia/Kings Canyon and only a couple hours' drive south from Stockton.

San Jose, 65 miles southwest of Stockton, has become the third-largest city in California. Among its intriguing attractions is the *Winchester Mystery House,* built over nearly four decades at the orders of an eccentric heiress, and containing 160 rooms, 2,000 doors, and 10,000 windows. Winding Highway 17 takes you to the *Boardwalk Amusement Park* and the Municipal Pier of **Santa Cruz**, at the northern cusp of Monterey Bay. Under decent driving conditions, the 100-mile trip to Santa Cruz takes two hours. Varied campgrounds are located nearby, such as *Henry Cowells Redwoods State Park* and *Big Basin Redwoods,* along with camp sites on the ocean, such as *New Brighton, Sunset,* and *Seacliff.*

All along the blue, crescent-shaped Monterey Bay lie the charms of dazzling beaches and cypress-covered hills. Across the bay you find quaint Carmel, the vistas of the *17-Mile Drive,* tranquil *Pacific Grove,* and scenic *Monterey.* The drive from Stockton to the **Monterey Peninsula** takes around 2½ hours. Monterey's *Cannery Row,* made famous by writer John Steinbeck (himself born and raised in nearby Salinas), now contains restaurants, galleries, and shops. Inarguably the greatest draw of the Peninsula is the world-class *Monterey Aquarium,* the largest in the world, containing 5,500 sea creatures. A tank holding a kelp forest that is 28 feet deep can be seen by viewers at top and bottom. Another tank 90 feet long holds a third of a million gallons of water. Open ocean fish such as shark and bat rays and porpoise swirl through it, to the fascination of viewers.

Splendid views of the Bay Area are accessible from two mountain tops, provided your auto doesn't object to tough climbs: from *Mount Diablo* in Contra Costa County, and from *Mount Tamalpais* in Marin County. On a clear day Mount "Tam" unfurls all of San Francisco and the East Bay, the lower peninsula, and the north coast—almost too much to take in.

The **Lower Peninsula** encompasses *Half-Moon Bay,* with its broad stretches of beaches; *Palo Alto,* home of Stanford University; *San Mateo,* and a dozen other cities linked like beads on strings along routes below San Francisco. The busy *San Francisco International Airport* borders U.S. 101, the Bayshore Highway, and the bay itself at Millbrae, 20 miles south of the city proper.

The **East Bay** has its charms, too, whether in the interior hills of Lamorinda (Lafayette, Moraga, and Orinda) or on the slopes facing the bay in a network of cities stretching from Fremont and Hayward in the south to the tip of Richmond in the north. The major cities are **Oakland** and **Berkeley.** Oakland features *Jack London Square,* with its plethora of restaurants and shops, the recreation area of *Lake Merritt,* the *Port of Oakland,* and the *Stadium* and *Coliseum* where the Oakland Athletics and the Golden State Warriors play their home games. Berkeley is most known for its University of California campus, marked by its distinctive Campanile.

The **North Coast Area** takes in the plunging coastlines and moors around Bodega Bay, home of the filming of Hitchcock's *The Birds,* down to the stark *Point Reyes* headlands, then on to pleasant towns in the interior such as *Petaluma, Novato,* and *San Raphael.*

Marin County towns just across the Golden Gate Bridge include rustic *Mill Valley,* fashionable *Tiburon,* and picturesque *Sausalito.* A grand natural wonder nearby is *Muir Woods,* home of enormous coastal redwoods, some a thousand years old. A walk through Muir Woods is guaranteed to be good for the soul.

Now to **San Francisco,** the brightest gem, saved for last. The City—as natives refer to it—cannot possibly be covered in a day, or a week, for that matter. Therefore the approach should be incremental. Divide up the city into distinct parts and devote a day or part of a day to exploring each one. Then return again to finish your excursions. Within weeks or months—however much time on and off you have to spend—you'll get to know the city well. It's worth the effort. Among several possible methods, the one that follows divides the city into five large districts.

The first encompasses downtown, the Embarcadero, Russian Hill, and Nob Hill, thus combining business and cultural centers, sophisticated residential areas, and the waterfront.

Start with the eight beaux arts buildings of the *Civic Center,* especially *City Hall,* the *Opera House, Davies Symphony Hall,* and the *Veterans Memorial,* containing the *Museum of Modern Art.* Other edifices to visit include *St. Mary's Church* and the *Hyatt Regency,* and the *Transamerica and Ferry buildings.* Shops and restaurants are to be found in great number in famed *Chinatown*; around *Union Square,* including offshoot *Maiden Lane,* and along *Union Street*; at *Ghirardelli Square* and the *Cannery*; and at *Pier 39.* Bay cruises may be taken from the *Fisherman's Wharf* area out to the Golden Gate Bridge, around *Alcatraz* and *Angel Island,* and underneath the Bay Bridge. A refreshing day can be spent on the 12 miles of hiking trails around Angel Island, reachable only by ferry. Other tourist stops can include the *Balclutha,* a square-rigged sailing ship; the *Maritime Museum;* or the top of *Coit Tower,* and its panoramic views. Additional sightseeing in the district includes the *Japan Center* complex; a twisting ride in your car down *Lombard Street,* billed as "the crookedest street in the world"; lively *North Beach*; and the restfulness of *Washington Square* at Columbus and Union. Theaters, art galleries, other cultural attractions, restaurants, pubs, and stores abound in this district. Where available use *Cable Cars* and BART to get around.

District #2, to the northwest, starts in the Marina at *Fort Mason,* allowing for a tour of the World War II Liberty ship *Jeremiah O'Brien*; a stroll around the *Palace of Fine Arts,* and for the children (and adults), entry into the *Exploratorium,* where they can indulge in exciting hands-on scientific play. Then head for the *Presidio* and a tour of *Fort Point,* a military museum and look-out. The *Golden Gate Bridge,* directly above the fort, is open to foot traffic, strolling, or running. Then take a drive along the *Golden Gate Recreational Area* to *Lincoln Park,* with stops at small beaches along the way, at the graceful *Palace of the Legion of Honor,* home to French art treasures, and the nearby *Cliff House.*

Central District #3 takes in the Richmond district and presents all the glories of one of the great urban parks in the world, *Golden Gate Park,* and its many attractions: the *Conservatory of Flowers*; the *Academy of Sciences* that houses planetarium, aquarium, and natural history museum; the *Asian Art* and the *de Young museums*; the *Japanese Tea Garden*; the *Arboretum*; boating on *Stow Lake*; and a hike up *Strawberry Hill.* Golden Gate is truly a citizens' park. But a word of advice: places for play, relaxation, and picnics can be found with greater ease than parking spaces.

District #4 to the southwest embraces Sunset, Parkside, Jonestown, Ingleside, and part of the Mission. Take a tour of *Mission Delores,* which is more than 200 years old. Drive up to *Twin Peaks* for magnificent views in all directions. Visit the *San Francisco Zoo,* ranked among the top six zoos in the world. Make sure to see its modern primate center. Among other activities: take in the campus of San Francisco State University, have a picnic in Stern Grove, go boating on Lake Merced, sun yourself and swim at any of the beaches along the Great Highway.

The fifth and last tour, to the southeast, doesn't provide much to do in the Mission, Potrero, and Bay View districts, but it gives the visitor a chance to wander around huge *McLaren Park*; to take in an event—whether concert, rodeo, or exhibition—at the *Cow Palace*; and to see a football or baseball game at *Candlestick Park,* as long as the 49ers and the Giants continue to play there.

We can indeed be grateful for having so many cultural riches, such a wealth of entertainment and recreation, so much glittering natural beauty right outside our front doors. It's one of the rewarding advantages to living in the heart of bounteous Central California. So . . . happy treasure hunting.

The Port of Stockton continues to play a pivotal role in sustaining the region's level of productivity. Photo by Steve Pereira

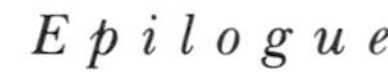

Into the Next Century

In the twenty-first century, Stockton-San Francisco, Stockton-Sacramento, and Stockton-Modesto will seem to draw closer, creating the impression, if not the fact, of a megalopolis. Merging will be most apparent along the corridors of Highways 580, 205, 5, 120, and 132 as housing developments and business centers respond to the lure of San Francisco and the Bay Area. The principal expansion will take place along South Stockton-Manteca-Lathrop-Tracy routes toward Altamont Pass. To a lesser extent, the same will be true as Stockton develops northward along 5 and 99 to join Lodi, both spreading onward beyond the San Joaquin County line toward Sacramento. Less expansion will likely occur to the south along highway corridors linking Stockton south toward Modesto.

These fine homes line the peaceful Meadow Lake. Photo by Mark E. Gibson

People don't go away, they multiply. Houses don't go away, they multiply. Cars don't go away, they multiply. Especially in California. The Los Angeles Basin and the San Fernando Valley, the Peninsula and Silicon Valley, all show the effects of overcrowding. Prospects for urbanization are echoing now over the Altamont down into the Central Valley. These overtures will be both welcomed and resisted, leaving many different planning decisions in their wake.

While growth is inescapable, it can also be manageable. In advance we should be creating new highways and arterial systems and building rapid transit lines. Otherwise traffic conditions will approach the gridlock intensity already plaguing the Los Angeles region and the Bay Area. Availability of water, sewer services, air quality, housing costs, quality of schools, and financial resources of the governing bodies are also important factors in planning. Unfortunately, it is human nature to delay and to try to recoup when the damage has already been done. Everyone will suffer from helter-skelter, catch-up attempts.

The growth of Stockton is already assured. The city proper should top the 200,000 mark around 1990. The Stockton metropolitan area that includes Lincoln Village, Morada, and other surrounding unincorporated districts will of course stay consistently larger; it's projected to reach 255,000 by 1990. By the turn of the century, Stockton metro will be nearly 300,000 inhabitants, and by 2020 well beyond a third of a million. These estimates predict an average increase of 30,000 residents per decade over the next three decades.

A much larger projection can be made for San Joaquin County. By 1991, its population will reach 483,000; by 1995, 556,000; by 2000, 612,000; and by 2020, 830,000. The increase in the county will thus average about 115,000 new residents per decade for three decades. (For purposes of comparison, the Census Bureau predicts that the population of California will increase to 29 million in 1990, 33.5 million in 2000, and 37 million in 2010.)

The ethnic makeup of Stockton stands at approximately 51 percent white non-Hispanic, 26 percent Hispanic, 15 percent Asian, and 8 percent black. City and county planners estimate that in the future Asian and black population will remain fairly stable at 15 percent and 8 percent. They foresee the Hispanic population leveling out at about 22 percent (the average throughout California is expected to be at least 20 percent), and the white non-Hispanic climbing to about 55 percent.

In the mid-1980s, an average of 2,431 legal immigrants settled annually in Stockton (specifically, 1,796 Asians, 449 Mexicans, and 186 of other nationalities). Asian is the fastest growing ethnic group, but Mexican is the largest group numerically. Economic betterment proved to be the main reason all of them came to Stockton.

The number of jobs in San Joaquin County reached 160,000 in 1987, excluding the self-employed and domestic help. Ranking for major employment should continue roughly in the current order and proportion: wholesale and retail trade jobs topping the list at 33,000; government jobs (including federal, state, county, and city) second at 30,500; followed by services at 30,000; manufacturing, 23,000; agriculture, 15,500; finance, insurance, and real estate, 9,000; transportation and public utilities, 8,500; construction, 8,000; and other, 2,500. Into the future, business and government jobs will likely hold their leading positions, manufacturing will continue to dominate over agriculture, and services will tend to stay ahead of manufacturing. Jobs are divided about evenly between white collar and blue collar, with a slight edge toward white collar. San Joaquin County presently ranks fifth in California in number of major businesses building new facilities or expanding existing ones.

Building is everywhere on Stockton's horizon.

Since the late 1970s, almost three-quarters of a million square feet of downtown commercial space have been renovated into banks, restaurants, stores, and offices. By the mid-1990s, additional renovation downtown will include the following: a transportation mall/transfer station for SMART (Stockton Metropolitan Area Rapid Transit); the completion of the eight-story American Savings Plaza, with a quarter-million square feet of office space and an underground parking garage, at a cost of $42 million; the five-story County Human Services Building, at a cost of $30 million; and city and county multi-story parking garages, adding a thousand parking spaces to current totals, at a cost of $11 million. These and a new senior citizens complex are all located within a 30-block downtown area scheduled to undergo continuing rejuvenation. Its boundaries extend from Miner to Washington streets, and El Dorado to Stanislaus streets.

New office towers and apartment complexes on the south shore of the Stockton channel and proposed development of the channel's north shore and Weber Point, to include construction of a major hotel/convention center, office buildings, apartments, restaurants, an amphitheater, and a complex of stores, stretch ahead in the 1990s. An architect's team in the early 1980s commented, "Revitalization is possible only through complementary economic and physical development coordinated with development plans in adjacent areas and with the total support of divergent downtown interests in a new public/private partnership."

Such development will be abetted by the continuation of the Crosstown Freeway linking Interstate 5 to Highway 99. That project is scheduled for completion in the early 1990s. Forecasts show 80,000 cars traveling on it daily.

A great building surge is projected in housing, to meet the needs of the anticipated thousands of new residents. Among the largest projects is the Weston Ranch, west of Interstate 5 between San Joaquin General Hospital and Van Buskirk Park. A total of some 2,000 acres of farmland, now annexed to the city, will contain almost 7,000 homes. Calling for a shopping center, parks, and schools, the project will involve 12 different phases, the last to occur past the turn of the century.

Two adjacent housing projects are proceeding on the northeast side of the city bordering West Lane. The 200-acre Weber Ranch adjoins the 150-acre Sperry Ranch.

To the north, Spanos Park, a residential and commercial development of nearly 1,300 acres, is to be built west and east of Interstate 5 between Bear Creek and Eight Mile Road. Some 7,500 homes are projected by the year 2010.

Brookside Community, on 1,200 acres in a square bordered by Fourteen Mile Slough, Ten Mile Slough, the Calaveras River, and Smith's Levee, will consist of more than 3,000 single and multi-family units, a retirement village, a hotel and conference center, parks, two lakes, and a golf course. The Grupe Company will continue the project into the twenty-first century.

Two other smaller housing projects are slated. Harbor Cove, south of Bear Creek, building to 1995, is slated by the Bassell Land company to cover 360 acres with more than 600 homes. It will be a gated community, with a boat dock for each home. In Morada an additional 320 acres, to contain 2,000 residential units, is being developed by Grupe.

In all, 16 subdivisions are expected to swell the Stockton metro population by 80,000 by the year 2020. Other projects call for continued expansion of the Stockton Auto Center and adjacent properties along Hammer Lane, and a 6,000-seat sanctuary, amphitheater, and chapel on more than 60 acres northeast of the Auto Center to be built by the Christian Life Center.

Barring recession or catastrophe, Stockton's economy is expected to undergo steady growth at most levels well into the next century. Global demands for farm products need to edge upward. Retail businesses are projected to grow at moderate rates; selective new industries and distribution centers should thrive. Stockton's strength will continue to be diversification. The fastest growth, which often gallops out of control, occurs in regions that have strong aerospace industries or defense industries; in their absence, Stockton can continue to regulate its annual growth at a reasonable 3+ percent.

San Joaquin County will likely resist efforts to have it become the 10th county in the 9-county Bay Area. Although ties to the Bay Area grow closer, San Joaquin County is far enough away and different enough to maintain its own identity, unlike, say, the Tri Valley (Livermore-Pleasanton-Dublin) that has been drawn irretrievably into the Bay Area net.

Clearly Stockton cannot afford some aspects of the growth that is being projected. Both city and county are no longer in a building mode; after all, federal, state, and local funds are much less plentiful than they used to be.

Transportation remains a key issue. If traffic worsens, Stockton becomes no different from other congested urban areas. North and south routes along Interstate 5 and Highway 99 are at peak times already outmoded. Although at its completion the Crosstown Freeway will alleviate congestion, it will not do enough for east-west routing. A wide arterial south of the airport between 5 and 99 is needed because of the several million square feet of warehouse space and other developments added in South Stockton. A wide arterial north of the city between 5 and 99, now in progress on Eight-Mile Road, has been deemed necessary because of added growth and housing development. Only by continued expansion of roads will Stockton metro be able to keep a handle on traffic problems; otherwise, by the early twenty-first century these problems threaten to become monumental.

Rapid transit is an important alternative. The retention of the Atchison, Topeka, and Sante Fe rail lines west of Stockton is essential for future rail service to Concord and Martinez. Southern Pacific and Union Pacific lines are also available over the Altamont to Livermore. Light rail might then be used to Dublin, where it could later be connected to BART. Four frequencies (train runs) on the San Joaquin between Bakersfield and Sacramento are now possible, according to Bill Sousa, a San Joaquin County supervisor. He foresees "high-speed rail [at 125 mph] in a few years, supplemented by state-of-the-art equipment." In the meantime, bus transportation provided by SMART can link up Stockton-Tracy-Dublin. It will likely be well into the next century before a rapid transit system from the Bay Area heads in this direction.

George Sangster, economic development director of the Stockton Chamber of Commerce, believes that Stockton is more recession-proof than geographically restrictive areas like San Francisco. While remaining bullish on Stockton, he has several concerns. Housing costs must be kept down, he says. If not, "We lose the very people who came here in the first place to escape high costs elsewhere."

About unemployment, he worries "that there won't be enough jobs to equal the new residents coming into the area." And he argues that the educational attainment level must be improved: "People need to be better educated to be employed." This position is echoed by other city and county officials who insist that good schools serve as a magnet to draw new families.

Among other issues that must continue to be addressed are:

(1) air quality—increased traffic and industry may produce pollution.

(2) sewer services—they must be adequate to meet growth needs for new housing and industries.

(3) water supply—it must be sufficient to satisfy domestic, industrial, and agricultural uses.

(4) air transportation—sufficient flights in all directions must be available to satisfy the public.

With respect to the last issue listed, a large regional airport to accommodate both Stockton and Modesto could answer these needs, if political and territorial differences between the two cities are resolved.

Gary W. Johnston, San Joaquin County extension director, is concerned about the eventual doubling of the county's population early in the next century and the subsequent loss of prime farmland. Also, he sees formidable challenges ahead for legislation on farm labor, the use of pesticides, and labor costs.

As the number of commuters who reside here increases, the number of businesses that move here subsequently increases. In other words, businesses tend to gravitate toward a large commuter base, in which case Stockton would directly benefit.

However, activist Dario Marenco expresses concern about businesses coming into Stockton from the outside. They tend not to be as successful as home-grown businesses, he claims. Marenco doesn't think growth will be as extensive as some have predicted. Our advantages, he says, are in our open space, our long established independence, and our diversification. The question remains whether Stockton will become urbanized or whether it will retain some of its provincial, even rural character.

Tom Walker, deputy director of planning for San Joaquin County, anticipates more plans for large, isolated developments, especially in the southern part of the county. These plans call for new communities ranging from 20,000 to 30,000 residents, to begin around the turn of the century.

Dave Schmidt, economic development coordinator for the City of Stockton, values the identification of problems as both instructive and constructive. Only then, he believes, can you prepare to attack them.

All agree that Stockton and the county must maintain a quality living environment. No one wants to see the quality of life here deteriorate. It is not enough simply to be larger. The plethora of problems brought on by the phenomenal recent growth of San Jose illustrates this point. While our situation in Stockton is promising and bright, we must be prudent and cautious. Then the manageable benefits of Stockton—affordable housing, open space, ample labor pool, convenient transportation network, and active economic development, to name a few—can remain benefits.

Quality of life matters most and should remain uppermost in our minds as we determine our future.

This young swimmer is cooling off in the city's public pool. Photo by Kerrick James

A cool evening sky colors this image from the Port of Stockton.
Photo by Steve Pereira

Part **2**

Stockton's Enterprises

Chapter 6

Networks

Stockton's communication providers keep information circulating within the area.

Photo by Steve Pereira

Continental Cablevision;
114

KJOY-AM and KJAX-FM;
115

Continental Cablevision

Continental Cablevision has long enjoyed a reputation as a well-managed, conscientious company.

That fact was brought home recently when Continental was ranked number one in quality of management in a survey of the top 25 multiple system operators by the industry publication, *CableVision.* Continental also ranked number one in quality of service, financial savvy, community relations, and the quality of its work environment.

The company's success has a lot to do with its basic principle that customer satisfaction is top priority. It is an ideal that has helped Continental grow in Stockton from a few subscribers when it first opened there in 1972 to a current figure of more than 47,000 subscribers.

Providing approximately 40 channels, Continental's economic impact on the city is considerable. In addition to its payroll, which has a ripple effect, the firm pays a franchise fee to the city of 5 percent of its gross revenues in addition to a 6-percent users tax on cable. Also, all 55 company vehicles are purchased from local dealers.

An aerial view of Continental's expansive plant on Tam O'Shanter in Stockton.

Continental's leadership is involved in a number of local organizations, ranging from the local arts to boys' and girls' clubs. United Way and other community agencies have presented Continental with awards of excellence for its contributions, including participation in United Way's loaned executive program.

Continental's first plant was located on West Lane, but it is now headquartered at 6505 Tam O'Shanter. The ultramodern facility incorporates some 20,000 square feet, which is home for roughly 150 office and technical personnel.

The firm is known as one of the area's better employers, as evidenced by the long tenure of many of its employees and a waiting list of potential employees. Two-thirds of the company's managers began in entry-level positions. In addition to the plant on Tam O'Shanter, Continental maintains a regional office in downtown Stockton.

In addition to Stockton, Continental offers cable service in Linden, Manteca, Fresno, Clovis, Madera, Hanford, Tulare, Reno, and Yuba City/Marysville. The corporation's headquarters is in Boston, where Continental is headed by Tim Neher and the chairman of the board, Amos Hostetter, Jr.

Continental's services are multifaceted. In addition to offering a full array of basic and premium channels, Continental can turn service on and off from the office or offer services on a pay-per-view basis. That is where the subscriber can order a particular program. In the case of a sporting event, for example, the subscriber simply orders the program. The company authorizes it. And, at the given time, the subscriber tunes in the particular channel to view the event.

Complex electronic equipment, such as this satellite dish, are constantly maintained to ensure high-quality home reception.

Continental also does the same thing with movies, which it gets at the same time they are offered at video stores. The subscriber simply has to order a film at a selected time and the program appears.

As for future developments, Continental Cablevision is continually looking at emerging technology, including fiber optics, which would allow the company to pass along many more channels with greater reliability.

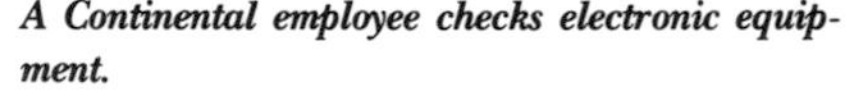

A Continental employee checks electronic equipment.

KJOY-AM and KJAX-FM

In virtually every city in the country there's a legendary radio station that entire generations grew up listening to. In Stockton, that radio station is KJOY. From the "Howdy Honkers" era of Rick Cimino and Ted Payne in the 1950s, when KJOY broadcast live from Shower's Drive-In, "Sixty-one-eleven Hamburger Heaven," on Friday nights and it seemed half the town was trying to figure out treasure hunt clues that would help them find KJOY's $10,000 hidden bank draft, to the KJOY Good Guys of the 1960s and continuing with popular personalities and fun contests through the 1970s and 1980s to today, KJOY has always been known for its fun, personality-oriented sound that has dominated Stockton radio for decades.

Originally KXOB, it was purchased by Joseph Gamble in 1953, and the call letters were changed to KJOY, "the smile on your dial," in 1956. Festivities commemorating the name change included a telegram from Richard Nixon and a reception featuring Don Sherwood, who was the most popular disc jockey of his time. The station facilities were moved from above a shop on Pacific Avenue's Miracle Mile to the transmitter site east of Highway 99, where, in the famous floods of the mid-1950s, employees had to use a rowboat to get to work, and the station broadcast in almost two feet of water for several days, in spite of constant pumping. The station was moved to the mezzanine of the historic Hotel Stockton in 1958, and has broadcast from the studios in the window on the corner of Weber and El Dorado since 1959.

In 1968 KJAX went on the air, resurrecting call letters the company had previously used on a station it owned in Santa Rosa, and became the county's only beautiful music station. It was known then as Cloud 99 for its relaxing music and offices high atop what was Stockton's tallest building at the time. As it evolved through the years into contemporary easy listening, KJAX became Stockton's most popular station in the 1980s.

Locally owned, the stations have been operated by the Gamble family for more than four decades. When Joseph Gamble died in 1963, his brother-in-law, Ort Lofthus, became general manager and ran the stations for more than 20 years before retiring in 1986. The tradition continues today with Gamble's son, Joel.

The historic Hotel Stockton building in the downtown area is home to KJOY-AM and KJAX-FM.

"Radio is an exciting and dynamic business," Gamble states. "It forms an emotional bond with the listener. People use radio as a companion, to reflect or change their mood, and to be entertained and informed." Its immense popularity and reputation as an excellent advertising value is due to several unique advantages, Gamble points out. "It is the only medium that can be enjoyed while doing something else; it goes everywhere you go and reaches people all day. And it's immediate," says Gamble. "When people want to find out what's going on, whether it's news, sports, weather, traffic, or something happening in the community, they turn to the radio.

"Radio also has the ability to not only inform people but persuade them, as well, by involving the listener's imagination to create a visual mental image that puts them in the picture," he says. "Because of this ability to communicate one-on-one, no media is more efficient at positioning and reinforcing an advertiser's image."

In the 1990s things are likely to continue to change. "In this business, about the only thing that's certain is change," Gamble notes. "You have to constantly evolve as the times and people's tastes change. Our goal is to continue to lead the market in adult listenership, in particular better-educated, affluent, upscale adults, and to be the best value now and in the future. To do this, we are constantly updating and refining our programming to continuously appeal to an ever-changing audience." One thing that won't change, however, according to Gamble, is the company's philosophy and commitment to strong community involvement, local news and sports, and fun major-market quality entertainment, personalities, and contests.

Chapter 7

Industry

Producing and distributing goods and foodstuff for consumers, industrial firms provide employment for many Stockton area residents.

Photo by Mark Gibson

Corn Products of Stockton; 118

American Moulding & Millwork Company; 120

Valley Electric Company; 122

Valimet Inc.; 123

Sharpe Army Depot; 124

Nestlé Foods Corporation; 126

Corn Products of Stockton

Corn Products of Stockton is one of those quiet companies that seldom makes the news. But the fact is, the firm is a major economic force in the community and turns out ingredients used in many of the public's most popular food products.

Corn Products is a unit of CPC International, Inc., which has annual sales of more than $4.5 billion, ranking it as one of the largest food companies headquartered in the United States, with some 100 plants in 47 countries.

Major consumer brands for which CPC is known include: Hellmann's and Best Foods mayonnaise, Mazola corn oil and margarine, Skippy peanut butter, Arnold breads, Thomas' English Muffins, Mueller's pasta products, Karo and Golden Griddle syrups, and Knorr soups, sauces, and bouillons. Corn Products in Stockton and in other U.S. plants provide ingredients for many of these products.

Corn Products has a dramatic impact on the economy of the San Joaquin Valley, and Stockton in particular. The plant, at 1021 Industrial Drive, is the second-largest consumer of California corn in the state. During the local harvest, when Corn Products purchases 15 percent of its annual corn needs, up to 80 trucks of corn per day are unloaded.

During the balance of the year 75 car trains of corn arrive weekly at the plant via the Union Pacific Railroad. This means almost 2 million pounds of corn are converted each day into 50 outbound trucks of product 365 days per year. More than 75 percent of this product is shipped within San Joaquin and other nearby counties.

The plant generates more than $15 million in local spending annually. Due to Corn Products' presence in Stockton, two other facilities have located at the site, creating an investment of more than $150 million on the corner of Industrial Drive and Airport Way.

Corn Products originally hired all of its operating personnel locally, and more than 90 percent are still with the company. The employees are salaried, nonunion, and participate in a gain-sharing bonus program.

The plant produces a 42-percent High Fructose Corn Syrup (HFCS), a nutritive, caloric sweetener used in canning, ketchup, baking, soft drinks, and other food industries, replacing beet and cane sugar; a 55-percent High Fructose Corn Syrup, a nutritive, caloric sweetener primarily used by such major brand soft drink manufacturers as Coca-Cola and Pepsi-Cola, as well as wine-based coolers such as California Cooler; industrial- and food-grade unmodified starch, used as a binder for the manufacture of paper and corrugated boxes; and a variety of dairy, beef, and poultry feeds, all by-products of the corn refining process. Statistics indicate that more than 250 million pounds of Corn Products' dairy feed is consumed annually within an average of 40 miles of the plant.

The market for HFCS was created in 1970, when the product was lit-

Each day 50 trucks leave Corn Products loaded with shipments of high-fructose corn syrup.

At Corn Products' master control room, an employee communicates on a direct phone line to Air Products and Chemicals' cogeneration plant, which supplies 40 percent of its steam and power to the giant corn refining plant.

tle more than a laboratory curiosity. Eighteen years later, in 1988, 15 billion pounds of HFCS was purchased by consumers.

Corn Products, the only corn-refining plant west of the Rocky Mountains, started up operations in April 1981, 18 months after construction commenced. The sophisticated, high-technology plant represented a dramatic departure from corn-refining plants built prior to the 1970s. Corn Products' sister plant in Argo, Illinois, was built in 1906 and as late as 1976 had thousands of workers to produce three times the output of the Stockton plant, which originally operated with a total work force just exceeding 50 people.

Now, after an expansion program, the Stockton plant operates with almost the same number of employees and requires only five people per rotating shift to run the entire operation 365 days per year. The balance of the work force includes truck and railroad loading and unloading personnel, and maintenance and office and management staff.

The difference between the Stockton facility and other older generation plants is capital. Multiple tens of millions of dollars in fixed assets, complete with process-control computer systems and instrumentation, vastly reduced the number of employees and substantially increased product quality and process reliability.

During the early 1980s energy became the plant's second-highest cost after corn. That was when the company decided to use the Federal Energy Regulatory Commission statutes and have Air Products and Chemicals build an environmentally safe, coal-fired cogeneration plant to supply Corn Products with steam and electricity. The multimillion-dollar cogeneration plant commenced operations in March 1988.

In order to safeguard the environment, APCI selected a state-of-the-art circulating fluidized bed boiler that minimizes air pollution emissions to a level significantly lower than conventional natural gas-fired boilers of similar size.

Furthermore, Corn Products of Stockton also spent millions of dollars to clean up already existing pollutant emission sources in the valley. Cogeneration will save the Stockton plant millions of dollars in annual operating costs, as well as supply electricity to Pacific Gas & Electric for its requirements.

BELOW: Corn Products is among the largest consumers of California corn in the state. The plant produces corn syrups and different grades of corn starch.

American Moulding & Millwork Company

Beginning in 1910 as a company making wooden boxes for California's farm produce industry, American Moulding & Millwork Company (then known as Stockton Box Company) has adapted to changing markets by skillfully balancing its marketing efforts with manufacturing capabilities.

The company was acquired by AMMC on May 15, 1987, and is a privately owned corporation that operates two facilities, one in Stockton and a sister plant in Prineville, Oregon. The Stockton facility is located on a 57-acre site adjacent to West Lane, south of Alpine Avenue, and houses the corporation's headquarters. The plant employs some 70 salaried and 360 hourly employees. Since the acquisition, significantly more capital has been spent on both the Stockton and Prineville operations in the first two years of operation under the new management than was spent in the previous six years. Such capital investments ensure the firm's future.

From its 57-acre site in Stockton, American Moulding & Millwork produces a large variety of products, including unfinished furniture, precision wood parts for other manufacturers, moulding and millwork for home use, and wooden containers for the agricultural industry.

The company processes roughly 130 million board feet of lumber annually, of which 60 million board feet is processed at the Stockton plant. The raw material handled at the Stockton plant is shipped in from the northern Sierras and sometimes from as far away as Washington.

The Portland shadow line ripsaw allows the operator to select the optimum rips from each board.

American Moulding & Millwork Company prides itself in producing precision wood parts for other manufacturers and the moulding and millwork seen in a typical home. This includes the mouldings around door jambs as well as the door jamb, the baseboards, the casing around the doors and windows, and crown mouldings that are sometimes used to accent ceilings. Other products include components for stile and rail doors, which are sold to the door manufacturers who assemble the parts. AMMC is the largest supplier of door component parts in the country. The Prineville operation also makes ready-to-assemble windows that are shipped to a "glazer," who assembles the wood components and installs the glass.

Along with moulding/millwork and wooden containers for the agricultural industry, the Stockton plant also manufactures unfinished ready-to-assemble pine furniture that is distributed in the United States, Japan, and Europe. These units are so precisely milled and accurately dimen-

After being cut to rough size and width, furniture parts are further machined by a tenoner.

Every day approximately 15,000 furniture parts are processed by the Kimwood Sander, which prepares the wood with the smooth surface needed for finishing.

sioned that upon arrival at home the consumer can be admiring his handiwork within an hour after removal from the carton. The furniture lines include armoires, dressers, desks and rolltops, nightstands, and other functional pieces for the bedroom. These products are marketed through the mass-merchandiser, home center stores, and discount warehouse clubs. The company is also positioning itself to market a finished line of furniture in the same ready-to-assemble package.

AMMC is still principally a producer of moulding and millwork products; however, there are many variables in the housing construction markets over which AMMC has no control. As a result, AMMC is not banking its future on this industry alone, but is looking toward the remodeling and repair market as well as the furniture and wood component industry, both of which continue to grow in sales. "We're trying to position our company in markets that aren't so sensitive to fluctuating interest rates. In doing so we believe that steady growth for both company and employees will result," states Bernie Sloop, president of AMMC.

Community involvement and concern for the employees' welfare are more than mere phrases with the owners and management of the company. Whether it be matching its employees' contributions to United Way or providing academic scholarships to the families of its employees, American Moulding & Millwork Company believes that its strength is derived from its interaction with both the community and its employees.

The philosophy of AMMC is to encourage employee involvement in the company, believing that its many employees bring with them a continuing flow of new ideas that can add to the firm's strength. "Without our employees, the company is nothing more than machines, structures, and property—an environment in which nothing can happen," states Sloop.

ABOVE: Furniture parts are carefully precleated before being packaged and shipped to mass-merchandisers and other retailers.

LEFT: A ready-to-finish armoire by American Moulding & Millwork is economical and gracefully styled.

Valley Electric Company

Its business roots are in supplying the basic electrical materials and equipment. But Valley Electric Company envisions its future to be in factory automation equipment.

The move to factory automation has not been a spur-of-the-moment decision. Valley Electric has been selling these high-technology products for more than 10 years, according to H. Lee Dempsey, Jr., who owns the company with his brother, Larry S. Dempsey.

Valley Electric owes its present excellent market position to Earl W. Raffety, who built what then was the C.H. Carter Company in 1921 into the Central Valley's largest electrical distributor and many years later gave the Dempseys their start.

The history of the firm was in nuts and bolts. But the Dempseys believed that unless they involved Valley Electric in the high-technology business, the company eventually would find itself confined to selling commodity items. "Then we would have been in trouble," Dempsey says. So the Dempseys have turned to, among other things, computer integrated manufacturing equipment, which links computers, manufacturing, and processing together to automate an entire plant.

"We think factory automation products will become 35 percent of our business," says H. Lee Dempsey. "Right now it is 10 percent."

Valley Electric distributes electrical supplies for the vicinity of Merced north to Yuba City. "We're pretty local," Dempsey explains. "We have 3,000 customers of which 1,500 are in Stockton alone."

The firm handles some 350 manufacturers' lines with some 28,000 different items, including electrical wiring and cables, conduit pipe, wiring devices, electrical distribution equipment, fixtures, lamps, and programmable controllers.

When Valley Electric, then the C.H. Carter Company, moved in the mid-1920s to Stockton, it had three employees who worked in a small building not far from where the company is located today at 945 East Lindsay Street. Unlike the cramped quarters of those early days, Valley Electric now occupies more than 110,000 square feet and employs some 120 people at three different sites, including Stockton, Sacramento, and Modesto. When the Stockton and Modesto operations were merged in the early 1980s, Valley Electric expanded its facilities at both locations to include a computer center for programmable controllers, as well as customer training.

Lee Dempsey attributes the firm's success to Raffety's policy of having a complete inventory to service the needs of all of the company's customers. "We're going to stay with what we know best—the wholesale distribution business," he says.

Lee Dempsey graduated from California Polytechnic State University with a bachelor of science degree in engineering. Larry Dempsey graduated from San Jose State with a bachelor of science degree in industrial management. Prior to becoming involved with Valley Electric Company, Lee Dempsey had been a field engineer for a national electrical manufacturer. Larry was a design engineer in the missiles and space division of the Lockheed Company.

ABOVE: With a new emphasis on factory automation equipment, Valley Electric Company enters the 1990s. The visionary leadership is provided by brothers Larry (seated) and Lee Dempsey, who serve as president and chief executive officer, respectively.

RIGHT: Wholesale is their business: vice-presidents John Milner (left), Tom Solari (seated), and Floyd Redmen.

Valimet Inc.

Valimet Inc., located at 431 Sperry Road, produces metal powders, but it is best known for its production of spherical aluminum powder used in the solid fuels that drive the space shuttle, rockets, and missiles.

Among the company's clients are some of the biggest names in the business: Aerojet General, Hercules Aerospace, and Morton Thiokol, Inc., all of which purchase the Valimet product and mix it to make solid fuels.

Valimet was founded in 1975 by owners William Fortman and Kurt Leopold, who based their operation on the idea of supplying special aluminum powders to other manufacturers. In addition to aerospace, there are many other uses for the aluminum powders, including as a mix in making special automotive paints.

Valimet also makes an aluminum silicon alloy powder by inert gas atomization. It is used to form an aluminum coating for stationary and moving parts in the hot turbine area on Pratt & Whitney Aircraft jet engines. The coatings are accomplished by diffusion in a pack-coating process. The resulting coating protects the parts from oxidation, erosion, and thermal fatigue.

Valimet currently does in excess of $6 million in sales annually but is headed toward the $10-million range, according to Fortman.

The company buys its raw aluminum ingots from such corporations as Reynolds, Alcoa, and Alcan. In order to atomize it, Valimet melts the metal and sprays it in a helium atmosphere where the tiny particles freeze very rapidly and become a fine dust. The Valimet atomization process enables production of closely controlled particle size ranges from one millimeter down to micron diameters. The generally usable sizes fall between minus 80 mesh (177 micron) down to five microns. Among the powders that can be shipped from stock on short notice are aluminum and a wide range of aluminum alloys.

Valimet employs between 50 and 75 people. There are 25,000 to 30,000 square feet under cover at the plant, which is situated on 18 acres northwest of Stockton Metropolitan Airport.

ABOVE: Valimet's aluminum atomizing system turns out up to 2 million pounds of product annually.

RIGHT: Magnified 200 times, these metallic spheres come from metallic powder, produced by a rapid solidification atomizing process.

Taking advantage of the mild climate of the Central Valley, Valimet is able to use its access to such nearby transportation facilities as airports, deep-water ports, and railroads to ship its products worldwide without seasonal interruptions.

With the exception of the metal purchases, Valimet circulates approximately $3 million in the community in terms of payroll and local purchases, according to Fortman.

Valimet has complete analytical laboratory facilities, employing state-of-the-art techniques for elemental analysis by Atomic Absorption Spectrophotometry.

The highly qualified laboratory personnel can provide data on physical characteristics, including density, shape, flow rate, and full-range particle size distribution by Microtrac, Coulter Counter, dry or wet sieve, Fisher Subsieve Sizer, or any other specified method.

Sharpe Army Depot

The key to the success of any military organization's mission is the performance of the dedicated military and civilian men and women who support and supply the operation. From the forklift operator to the computer clerk, from the packer to the security guard, these are the people who work together toward a common goal.

At Sharpe Army Depot the goal is one of excellence, involving a work force of nearly 1,200 civilians, 30 military personnel, and approximately 100 contract workers.

Sharpe Army Depot is one of three area-oriented depots with the major supply responsibility for an area that covers almost one-half the earth's surface. It performs extensive storage and distribution operations for supplies destined to installations in the eight westernmost states, including Alaska and Hawaii, as well as to Guam; Okinawa, Japan; and Korea.

In carrying out its mission, the depot receives, repairs, tests, preserves, packs, stores, and ships materiel to the Army and other branches of the armed services, as well as to designated international customers.

Meeting the future's challenge of force modernization, Sharpe Army Depot is streamlining its operation around a new 20-acre state-of-the-art distribution facility. The facility incorporates the latest technological advances in materiel handling and distribution, and consolidates more than 20 separate functions under one roof.

As part of the U.S. Army Depot System Command (DESCOM), Sharpe is one of 18 depots; there are 12 depots and 5 depot activities in the United States and one depot in Germany.

In January 1986 Sharpe began construction on a new, high-tech, 20-acre Western Distribution Facility geared to the 1990s and beyond, with estimates of more than one million customer shipments and almost an equal number of transshipments per year. The facility features the latest technological advances in materiel handling and distribution, and will consolidate more than 20 separate functions under one roof.

At 852,028 square feet, the quarter-mile-long, one-tenth-mile-wide main distribution center is larger than the Rose Bowl and longer than the passenger liner *Queen Mary.* The building incorporates a 64-foot-high Rack and Bin storage system with a capacity for 35,280 pallet loads in racks and 156,000 line items in bins, with 328 pallets and 1,008 tote loads in Highly Active storage.

Materiel-handling equipment includes 2.9 miles of in-floor towline, 2.5 miles of package and pallet roller conveyor, and 1,064 linear feet of tilt-tray sortation.

Materiel identification and tracking is accomplished by way of barcode input to the computer control system. The facility's computer automation provides real-time processing of documentation and controls intrafacility movement of materiels.

The Western Distribution Facility brings state-of-the-art computers, materiel-handling systems, and current distribution management control concepts that allow Sharpe's team of supply experts to get the job done faster and better than ever before.

Sharpe is strategically located on 724 acres at the junction of the San Joaquin and Sacramento valleys, seven miles south of Stockton. The fa-

Gearing up for the 1990s and beyond, Sharpe Army Depot employees work together with computer-controlled materiel identification and tracking systems in the Western Distribution Facility's Highly Active storage area. Photo by Leroy Davis

Employees discuss stock transitioning procedures in Sharpe's new Distribution Facility's Rack and Bin area. The 64-foot-high Rack and Bin storage system is capable of storing more than 35,000 pallet loads in racks and 156,000 line items in bins. Photo by Leroy Davis

cility includes roughly 8 million square feet of improved storage space, with some 2 million covered and one-half million in controlled humidity warehousing.

Stockton is also the site of Sharpe's Watercraft Section, the Army's West Coast storage center for watercraft. Rough & Ready Island, the only one of its kind in DESCOM, has 540,000 square feet of water area available for the storage of watercraft. The facility is capable of preserving, storing, receiving, and shipping all types of floating craft and amphibious equipment.

In addition to its major supply mission, Sharpe Army Depot serves as the consolidation and containerization point for its area of responsibility. Supplies from the Army, the Defense Logistics Agency, the General Services Administration, and other sources are consolidated in air freight and sea-van containers and sent to customers in Alaska, Hawaii, and the Pacific.

As part of the "Total Army" concept, Sharpe Army Depot provides training for active reserve and National Guard units. A million-dollar, 15,000-square-foot training center barracks provides administrative space and sleeping accommodations for 100 soldiers on weekend and extended training missions.

Situated between Highway 99 and Interstate 5, the depot's location is strategic to California's major highway system. Highways, both north-south and east-west, provide access to regularly scheduled truck lines and contract carriers. Sharpe also has its own 3,200-foot-long airstrip, which is capable of handling the entire range of Army aircraft plus the Air Force's C-130 cargo plane.

The depot's tire receiving, storing, and shipping operation supplies its customers with tires and tubes ranging from bicycle to 2,000-pound construction equipment tires.

Sharpe Army Depot's significant work load and commitment to its employees places it in a key position for supporting the San Joaquin region today and into the twenty first century.

One of Sharpe's many missions is the maintenance of air delivery items and personnel parachutes for depot stocks and the Western United States, Alaska, Pacific, and Far East Commands. Photo by Leroy Davis

Nestlé Foods Corporation

Nestlé Foods Corporation produces and markets quality food and beverage products such as Toll House morsels, Nestlé Crunch, Nescafé and Taster's Choice coffees, Nestlé Quik, Nestea teas, Libby's Juicy Juice, and Kern's products. Many of these brands have been a part of American life-styles for more than 50 years.

The Nestlé legacy traces its roots back to Switzerland in 1866, when Henri Nestlé, a German chemist, formulated a milk food for infants unable to take mothers' milk. Nestlé established a business to produce and market his formula, and he subsequently produced sweetened condensed milk. In 1875 Daniel Peter, a chocolate manufacturer in Switzerland, combined his chocolate with Henri Nestlé's sweetened condensed milk and created the world's most popular confection—milk chocolate.

In the 1900s Nestlé opened its first American manufacturing plant in New York State for the production of Nestlé's milk food. In 1929 the facility in Ripon, California, was originally purchased to manufacture condensed milk. In 1938 Nestlé invented the technology for Nescafé instant coffee, and by 1948 the Ripon plant was manufacturing Nescafé. In the late 1970s Nestlé created a process to naturally decaffeinate coffee using water and coffee oils. The Ripon plant was the first Nestlé Foods factory to produce decaffeinated coffee with this unique process.

Coffee processed by Nestlé comes from such areas of the world as Central and South America and Africa. After its arrival at the plant, the raw coffee is checked for quality and blended according to Nestlé standards. Then it is roasted, ground, percolated, and, after being spray dried, packaged.

Today the Ripon factory manufactures Nescafé Classic, Nescafé Mountain Blend, Mountain Blend Decaffeinated, and Sunrise coffees. Decaffeinated products now use beans that have already been naturally decaffeinated.

The Nestlé Foods Corporation factory is the second-largest employer in Ripon. For more than 50 years the Nestlé plant has been active in the community by supporting the United Way, the chamber of commerce, and the Rotary Club. In addition, Nestlé employees have participated as members of the Volunteer Fire Department, in Almond Blossom festivities, and in Main Street Day. The plant's citizenship in the community has been demonstrated over the years through donations to the physical fitness center, the local fire department, the library, the senior citizen's center, and the Ripon recreation department. The plant also provides a series of science films to the Ripon school district each year.

Senior lab technician Glen Mapes checks the quality of incoming green coffee beans.

ABOVE: Nestlé's facility in Ripon, home of Nescafé Mountain Blend Instant Coffee.

RIGHT: Lift operator Thys De Hoop places incoming green coffee into a receiving and storage warehouse.

Photo by John Elk III

Chapter 8

Business and Professions

Stockton's business and professional community brings a wealth of service, ability, and insight into the area.

Photo by John Elk III

City of Stockton Office of Economic Development; 130

Chicago Title; 131

Greater Stockton Chamber of Commerce; 132

Neumiller & Beardslee; 134

Central State Credit Union; 136

Daugherty & Company Insurance Brokers, Inc.; 138

Diehl, Steinheimer, Riggio, Haydel & Mordaunt; 140

Feldman, Waldman & Klein; 142

Grant Thornton; 143

City of Stockton Office of Economic Development

Economic development is the lifeblood of a community, providing the new jobs and economic resources that are essential to the growth and vitality of a city.

The City of Stockton has continued to define and strengthen its own role in the economic development process, and to serve as a catalyst for economic growth. Indeed, much has been accomplished:

—A 25-member Citizens Economic Development Advisory Committee was appointed by the city council in 1983 to provide ongoing advice and recommendations to the city council.

—The city and its redevelopment agency have continued to move forward on a major, 70-acre waterfront development project on the south bank of the city's downtown waterfront. Detailed plans for development of other areas of the waterfront are also being prepared. The city's Redevelopment Agency also plays an active and aggressive role in revitalizing older areas of the downtown.

—In 1985 the position of Economic Development Coordinator had been established in the City Manager's Office to strengthen the city's role in and response to the needs of new industrial growth. In this capacity the Economic Development Coordinator works closely with the Greater Stockton Chamber of Commerce and San Joaquin County Economic Development Association.

—An Economic Development Review Committee was established within the framework of city government to provide a one-stop shop for the review of major new projects. The Economic Development Review Committee provides a mechanism to identify and resolve potential constraints, while providing a clear definition and overview of the city's regulatory process.

—The City of Stockton has continued to support a nationally recognized entrepreneurship training program, the Stockton Business Development Program, which has assisted in the creation of more than 40 small businesses.

—The city has co-sponsored an annual Minority Trade Fair and has worked with other organizations to publish a *Minority- and Women-owned Business Directory*.

—In 1986 the City of Stockton established a locally designated Enterprise Zone, providing a comprehensive set of investment incentives and development tools designed to attract new investments and create jobs in the city's central core.

With its excellent location, efficient transportation facilities, and relatively low land and labor costs, Stockton continues to attract more than its share of new industrial development. New residents from the Bay Area have also contributed to the city's dynamic growth.

Stockton also continues to strengthen and expand its cultural and economic links with other cities and countries of the Pacific Rim. Stockton currently has four sister cities, including Empalme (Mexico), Iloilo (Philippines), Shimizu (Japan), and Foshan (Peoples Republic of China). These relationships complement the city's ethnic and cultural diversity.

Stockton remains a place where east and west meet, and a place where the city's rich history is but a prologue to future accomplishment.

Stockton's south shore waterfront, along with the north shore and the downtown area, will become one homogeneous unit under the Central Stockton Plan, a quarter-million-dollar revitalization design effort drafted by architectural planners Kaplan McLaughlin Diaz.

Chicago Title

From its offices at 4612 McGaw Street in Stockton, Chicago Title takes a progressive approach to providing title and escrow services for the city's resale real estate and development communities.

Chicago Title's employees embody the firm's philosophy of professionalism, responsiveness, and friendliness.

The name may be midwestern, but its history as a Stockton company and its employees' dedication to the community make Chicago Title a Stockton firm in every sense of the word.

Founded in the late 1800s as a mom-and-pop operation with a very different name, the local office of Chicago Title has undergone numerous name changes as it has grown over the years. In more recent times it was known as Security Title and, later, Safeco Title before being bought out by Chicago Title in January 1987.

A full-service title company with offices at 4612 McGaw Street and branch offices in Lodi and Tracy, Chicago Title offers land title searches, land title guarantees, and a complete line of escrow services.

Chicago Title's philosophy is one of professionalism, responsiveness, and friendliness. For even though Chicago Title is a part of a much larger company, its employees are local residents who not only live in the community but contribute to it. Yet, at the same time, the local office is a part of a nationwide network that can help a client anywhere in the country.

The Stockton office features the latest in high-technology equipment, and its sophisticated computer system is tied in with a new $40-million system that was designed for Chicago Title's nationwide offices by the consulting firm of Arthur Anderson & Co. The system is used for all escrow work as well as in the title department and in preparing documentation.

The modern 10,000-square-foot office in which Chicago Title is located is owned by the company and was built more than eight years ago. It replaced an older downtown office.

Since becoming Chicago Title in 1987, the local office and its 33 employees have taken a progressive approach toward becoming the main provider of title and escrow services for Stockton's resale real estate community and some of the larger builders in the area.

With its corporate headquarters in Chicago, Illinois, Chicago Title's Stockton office is a part of the firm's Western Region, which is headquartered in Pasadena. The region includes Alaska, Arizona, California, Hawaii, and Nevada.

Greater Stockton Chamber of Commerce

Since 1901 the Greater Stockton Chamber of Commerce has been a driving economic force in the Stockton/San Joaquin community.

With a mission "to preserve and aggressively promote a strong local economy for the overall well-being of the area," the Greater Stockton Chamber of Commerce combines dedicated volunteer involvement with a professional staff working together to make things happen.

Historically economic development has been—and is—the keystone of chamber volunteer efforts. This economic development comes in many phases, starting with the attraction of new and encouragement of expanding industries.

While professional staff members coordinate the response to industrial inquiries, several chamber committees keep up the work of making Stockton/San Joaquin a good place in which to do business.

An ongoing effort in the legislative arena demands much of the chamber's attention. City, county, regional, and state government efforts that could assist—or hinder—business are the focus of special task forces. Since the Greater Stockton Chamber of Commerce relies on no public funds, it represents a much stronger voice of business in local and state legislative halls.

The chamber approaches economic generation in a number of productive ways. Service to existing industry is responsive to those established firms seeking to grow and prosper in the western economy. Community recognition and acknowledgement of the contribution of industry in investment and employment is annually sponsored through the chamber.

Since the early 1950s the Greater Stockton Chamber of Commerce has attracted several million

Fireworks burst above a football game at the University of the Pacific, California's oldest land grant college. Photo by Steve Pereira

Agriculture and water recreation meet in the 1,000 miles of waterways of the San Joaquin Delta. Photo by Steve Pereira

Stockton's skyline rises from the terminus of the Stockton Deepwater Channel. Photo by Steve Pereira

This tomato-processing line is an example of the high-tech agriculture that is a mainstay of the local economy. Photo by Steve Pereira

"new" dollars to the area through film production. The area offers a wide variety of film possibilities, plus an eager and ever-present pool of extras available to filmmakers.

Recognition of the importance of agriculture to the rich Central Valley brought the establishment of Stockton Ag Expo, which annually exhibits the latest in agricultural equipment and services during a three-day show at the expansive San Joaquin County Fairgrounds.

The chamber has picked up on the recreational attributes of the 1,000 miles of delta waterways with headwaters in Stockton. The five-day RV, Sports, and Boat Show annually attracts thousands to the historic waterfront area that was the major supply point to the southern goldfields during the gold rush of 1849.

As a nonprofit business corporation, the Greater Stockton Chamber of Commerce draws a great percentage of its support from volunteer membership investments. A 25-member board of directors gives of its time in establishing policy guidelines, while more than 25 percent of the some 2,000 member firms have direct involvement in a host of committees and task forces.

Recognized as one of the most active chambers in the state of California, the Greater Stockton Chamber of Commerce creates a number of opportunities for its investing members to generate new business.

Many special events dot the annual planning calendar delivered to each member every year. Events include business mixers, tennis and golf tournaments, Executive Connections, special recognition barbecues, motivational breakfasts, and formal affairs. As a service to members, the Greater Stockton Chamber of Commerce consistently offers a series of workshops and seminars ranging from the basics in business to more sophisticated workshops.

As its contribution to the future of the community, the Greater Stockton Chamber of Commerce was the first chamber in California to offer a year-long leadership development course. Leadership Stockton annually gives some 25 established and emerging leaders a comprehensive background and enlightened overview of what makes Stockton tick and what it takes to keep it ticking. A special, concentrated version of Leadership Stockton has been developed to give newcomers to the Stockton community a 12-hour "blitz" update and briefing on the area.

Recognizing the importance of small business as a growth industry, the Greater Stockton Chamber of Commerce addresses much volunteer and staff attention to the concerns of those who make up more than 50 percent of chamber membership. The organization's Small Business Council directs its concerns to both legislative and technical needs of small businesses.

While the dozens of volunteers and hundreds of business and professional members furnish both the person power and the financing for the ever-growing programs of the Greater Stockton Chamber of Commerce, the continuity and thrust comes from a professional staff of 14.

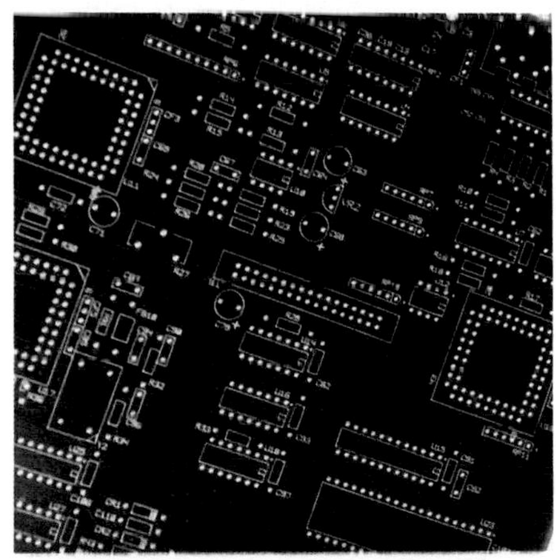

Circuit boards are just one of the many products manufactured by the high-tech industries that have relocated to the Stockton/San Joaquin Valley area. Photo by Steve Pereira

The single most important recognition of the balance of the Greater Stockton Chamber of Commerce program is that the organization has for 15 years met the national criteria to continue as one of the 600 local chambers throughout the United States recognized as an Accredited Chamber of Commerce.

Neumiller & Beardslee

The law firm of Neumiller & Beardslee, founded in 1903 by Charles L. Neumiller and George Ditz, employs more than 20 attorneys and represents major businesses, corporations, and institutions throughout Northern California.

A professional corporation, Neumiller & Beardslee was the first and is the largest and most diversified full-service law firm in the Stockton area. The firm's attorneys are specialists rather than general practitioners.

Major clients include The Grupe Co., ranked as one of the largest privately held real estate developers in the United States; Stockton East Water District; Delicato Vineyards; and St. Joseph's Medical Center.

As counsel for the Stanislaus River Flood Control Association, Neumiller & Beardslee was deeply involved in the successful 20-year fight to secure the construction and filling of New Melones Dam. The firm also was involved in the formation and serves to this day as general counsel for the Stockton East Water District, the largest purveyor of agricultural and municipal water in San Joaquin County. In particular, Neumiller & Beardslee was instrumental in working with the district in the construction of Stockton's municipal water-treatment plant.

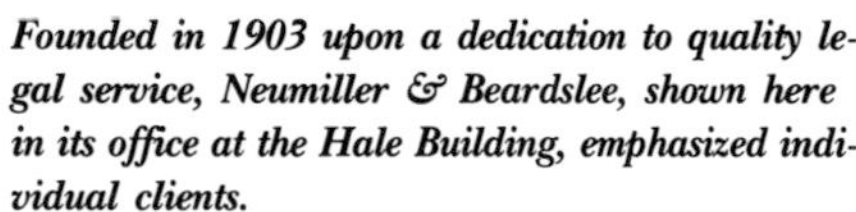

Founded in 1903 upon a dedication to quality legal service, Neumiller & Beardslee, shown here in its office at the Hale Building, emphasized individual clients.

Today Neumiller & Beardslee serves its commercial clients from its headquarters in the Waterfront Office Towers II at 509 West Weber Avenue.

Neumiller & Beardslee is built around the idea of personal service and prompt, dedicated, technically competent work with attention to detail. Owing to the nature of its practice, many of Neumiller & Beardslee's dealings are with law firms in the San Francisco and Los Angeles areas.

All of this is in contrast to the operation when Neumiller & Beardslee first opened. In those days Stockton was a small community, and the firm generally represented individual clients.

Neumiller & Beardslee occupies the better part of two floors in the Waterfront Office Towers II at 509 West Weber Avenue. Its partners include Thomas J. Shephard, Sr., Duncan R. McPherson, Rudy V. Bilawski, Robert C. Morrison, James R. Dyke, James A. Askew, John W. Stovall, Steven A. Herum, and Richard M. Archbold. Robert L. Beardslee, now counsel, remains active in the firm.

There have been close ties between the firm and the community, both on a professional and per-

From left to right are James R. Dyke, Duncan R. McPherson, Thomas E. Jeffry, Jr., and Steven D. Crabtree.

sonal level. Neumiller & Beardslee attorneys have served as chairmen, presidents, and members of the Greater Stockton Chamber of Commerce, San Joaquin County Bar Association, St. Joseph's Medical Center, San Joaquin County Board of Education, San Joaquin County Economic Development Association, Lassen Volcanic National Park Foundation, Yosemite Natural History Association, and the State Bar of California.

That kind of community activity goes back to Charles Neumiller, who was active in the Republican Party and served on the state prison board for a number of years. Over the years other firm members have been involved in both the Republican and Democratic central committees.

When the company first opened, Stockton was a small farming community. Charles L. Neumiller worked at the Farmers Union Milling Co. (later Sperry Flour Co.) and studied law at night. Eventually he was graduated from Hastings College of Law in 1901.

After a year as an assistant district attorney to District Attorney Arthur Ashley, Neumiller and Ashley founded Ashley & Neumiller. The partnership was dissolved in 1910. Five years later Neumiller and George Ditz, who went on to become a trustee of Stanford University, formed Neumiller & Ditz. The law office, which started out in Hunter Square and later was moved to the Hale Building at Main and Sutter streets, was shifted to the Commercial Savings & Loan Building, later the Bank of America Building.

Between 1913 and 1924 the firm's associates included Edward E. Breitenbucher, later a police judge, and David Lyman, who left to start an accounting firm. Irving Neumiller, a nephew of the firm's founder, became a partner in 1925, followed by Robert Beardslee in 1941.

In 1945 Dudley Sheppard joined the firm, and it became known as Ditz, Beardslee & Sheppard. Later the names of other partners were added to the name. But in 1972 the name was cut to Neumiller & Beardslee, and the offices were moved to 6 South El Dorado Street, where it remained until 1983, when it moved to its current offices in the Waterfront Office Towers.

The law firm helped to organize the Holt Manufacturing Co., which was incorporated in 1908 in Stockton and was a forerunner of the Caterpillar Tractor Co.

The firm also represented the Western Pacific Railroad, now the Union Pacific Railroad, in its efforts to serve Stockton. Southern Pacific unsuccessfully opposed Western Pacific's efforts.

Today the attorneys who make up Neumiller & Beardslee expect the company to grow while continuing to offer a full range of services to the people and businesses it serves. That belief is based on the expectations that San Joaquin and Stanislaus counties will continue to experience extensive growth in the next 20 years.

Professionally and personally, Neumiller & Beardslee attorneys maintain close ties to the Stockton community. At a local benefit are (from left): Robert C. Morrison, James A. Askew, Jeanne Zolezzi and Rudy V. Bilawski.

Central State Credit Union

At the helm of Central State Credit Union are vice-president Sharon McClelland (left) and president Willard Miller.

With some 10,000 members and 17 employees, Central State Credit Union is the second-largest credit union in San Joaquin County. Its assets, $33 million, place it among the top 11 percent of the credit unions nationwide.

Located at 919 North Center Street, Central State has enjoyed a close association with Stockton for more than 50 years. It has faithfully served state employees in San Joaquin, Stanislaus, Tuolumne, Amador, Solano, Calaveras, Alpine, Merced, and Mariposa counties since it was chartered in 1936.

Central State Credit Union's philosophy is: There are no customers, only members. And it is the membership that owns the credit union.

The credit union actively seeks new members, those who may not have had the opportunity to avail themselves of the services of a credit union. Originally limited to state employees, Central State's bylaws were amended a few years ago to include non-state employee members. Today that includes some 70 groups, ranging from the Stockton Board of Realtors to the San Joaquin County Dental Society, in addition to many individual employee groups.

The main criteria for membership is that the group not be currently affiliated with any other credit union. One exception to this practice was the 1985 merger of the University of the Pacific credit union with Central State. UOP membership includes the faculty and student body of the Stockton campus, along with the McGeorge School of Law in Sacramento and the School of Dentistry in San Francisco.

Willard E. Miller is president of Central State Credit Union. Sharon McClelland serves as vice-president. There is a seven-member board of directors. Every year two or three board seats become available, and any member can run for office. In addition, there is a credit committee. If a loan is turned down, the member can appeal to the credit committee. The credit union's management believes that recourse sets it apart from banks and savings and loan institutions. There is also an elected supervisory committee that performs an important audit/oversight function.

Central State offers low interest rates on loans and pays competitive rates on savings. In fact, Central State offers virtually every service offered by a bank except commercial loans, and that is by design. Those available services range from automobile loans on both new and used cars to equity loans. Members also can avail themselves of Visa cards with no annual fee and a 25-day grace period, so that the cardholder can pay off the balance without paying a finance charge.

A Gold automated teller machine card provides access to literally thousands of ATMs worldwide. Again, the card is issued at no cost to the credit union member, and there is no annual fee.

Offering membership in Central State Credit Union is easy. The sole criteria, whether an employee group or association, is that the organization not be affiliated with any other credit union. All it takes is filling out a one-page application, which is sent to the Department of Corporations. That agency regulates the credit union and must approve applications to offer membership to any new group. The process usually takes a week. Once an individual has joined, membership is open to other members of the family.

For the employer whose employees wish to join, offering membership in Central State costs nothing to the employer, and there are no employer obligations. What it does

provide the employer with is a fringe benefit for the employees. All it takes for an individual to join is a one-dollar membership fee and a minimum of $50 to open a share account. Accounts are insured up to $100,000 by the National Credit Union Administration Share Insurance Fund.

Because the credit union's charter encompasses nine counties, many transactions are conducted via mail and telephone. Central State maintains a toll-free 800 number and an in-house data-processing system. If members desire to conduct business from the privacy of their own homes, they merely have to push in the right code numbers and they can carry out any transaction, no matter what time of the day or night.

Central State occupies the lower floor of one wing of a 35,000-square-foot, two-story building it owns on Center Street. The building currently is in the process of being remodeled to provide more office space for Central State, which also has a small office on the campus of the University of the Pacific.

***From left to right:** Joe Montes, data coordinator; **Michael Hausenfleck**, assistant vice-president/loan services; **Sharon Evard**, assistant vice-president/member services; and **Michele Duclo**, assistant vice-president/accounting.*

Central State Credit Union is open Monday through Thursday from 9 a.m. to 5 p.m. and on Fridays from 10 a.m. to 6 p.m.

Daugherty & Company Insurance Brokers, Inc.

Daugherty & Company's board of directors (from left): Robert Perasso, William Scott, Marvin Daugherty, Scott Daugherty (president), Linda Music, and Doug Dinjian.

Daugherty & Company Insurance Brokers, Inc., is the oldest continually operated independent insurance agency in California. The agency, located at 2495 West March Lane, specializes in commercial lines insurance and also maintains fully staffed departments in surety bonds, employee benefits, and personal lines insurance.

An important element in the agency's continued success has been its commitment to providing the best-possible service to its clients. A staff of more than 30 technically skilled and professional employees provides Daugherty & Company's clients with a high level of service. By establishing relationships with major carriers, the agency has access to the complete spectrum of insurance products available in the industry. Daugherty & Company is licensed in 21 states, including Hawaii, and has agreements to transact business in all other states.

The agency traces its ties with Stockton back to 1852, when Lewis M. Cutting, the agency's founder, first arrived in the city. In 1857 Cutting became secretary and property manager to Captain Charles M. Weber, Stockton's founder.

Cutting opened his own real estate firm in 1860 at the corner of Bridge Place and Hunter Street. By 1885 Cutting's son, Francis, had joined him, and the agency was known as L.M. Cutting and Son. Lewis Cutting died in 1924, and his son continued in the business until 1953, when it was sold to Jack Curnow and William Scott.

In 1959 Curnow and Scott merged their agency with the Charles F. Thompson Insurance Agency, owned by Thomas Maguire and Marvin Daugherty, and the newly merged company became Cutting-Thompson Real Estate and Insurance.

In 1984 Scott Daugherty, son of Marvin Daugherty, became sole shareholder in the agency, and the name was changed to Daugherty & Company Insurance Brokers, Inc. Scott Daugherty began his career in insurance in 1973 with Fireman's Fund in San Diego after his graduation from San Diego State University. He subsequently joined the Cutting-Thompson agency in 1976.

Property and casualty brokerage at Daugherty & Company is the responsibility of the following account executives:

In addition to serving as Daugherty & Company's president and chief executive officer, Scott Daugherty is account executive to a large number of the agency's clients.

Doug Dinjian joined Daugherty & Company in 1981. Prior to joining the agency, Dinjian was general manager of Continental Restaurant Systems. He holds the CIC designation of the Society of Certified Insurance Counselors.

Continuing a family tradition, Jeff Daugherty joined the agency in 1979. Daugherty's specialty is insurance programs tailored for the agriculture industry.

Linda Paige has been with Daugherty & Company since 1983. With more than 20 years' experience in the insurance industry, Paige is a strong contributor to the agency's technical expertise.

Greg Van Ness joined the agency in early 1988, following a career in industrial real estate broker-

Agency president Scott Daugherty with his father, Marvin Daugherty.

The managerial team includes (from left): Vaughn Rogers, personal lines; Renie Kudenov, commercial lines; and Susan DeCicco, office manager.

age in the Stockton area and management consulting for a *Fortune* 500 holding company in New York City.

Dennis Nugent serves as new business coordinator for Daugherty & Company. His responsibilities include setting appointments with new contacts as well as servicing his own book of business.

Daugherty & Company uses advanced technology to provide the most efficient service possible. An automated rating department provides detailed, accurate quotes and greatly improves the processing of new business submissions with the agency's numerous insurance companies. A sophisticated computer system tracks account information, from policy lists to claims to detailed accounting data.

Service to Daugherty & Company's commercial lines accounts is provided by a staff of highly trained, professional customer service representatives, who are responsible for all aspects of the client's insurance program. The CSR acts as liaison between the client and the insurance company, and, in this role, greatly facilitates claims processing and other administrative details that would be cumbersome and time consuming for the client to handle directly.

The Commercial Lines Department administrative staff is supervised by Renie Kudenov, who joined the agency in 1984. Kudenov is also responsible for servicing the agency's largest accounts, and works directly with Scott Daugherty on complex new submissions.

The Personal Lines Department provides brokerage services for home owner, auto, boat, renter, and other personal lines policies to its accounts. Vaughn Rogers, who holds the prestigious insurance industry designations of CPCU and AAI, manages the Personal Lines CSRs, who perform the same valuable services to their accounts as do their counterparts in the Commercial Lines Department.

Robert Perasso heads the Employee Benefits Department at Daugherty & Company, which specializes in group medical and dental programs. Perasso was a successful life insurance producer before joining Daugherty & Company in 1983.

Daugherty & Company is one of the few insurance agencies that provides a fully staffed Surety Bond Department. Headed by Linda Music, who is also the agency's controller, the department provides brokerage services for all types of surety bonds, including contractor, subdivision improvement bonds, performance and labor and material bonds, bid bonds, and licensing bonds, as well as a wide variety of miscellaneous bonds. Scott Daugherty is president of the corporation's board of directors. Other directors include Marvin Daugherty, secretary; William Scott, vice-president; Robert Perasso; Doug Dinjian; and Linda Music.

Daugherty & Company serves its clients from offices located at 2495 West March Lane.

Diehl, Steinheimer, Riggio, Haydel & Mordaunt

From left to right are Michael Mordaunt, Mark Ornellas, Pam Lillard, William Horsey, Jr., and Richard Clarkson.

For more than 15 years Diehl, Steinheimer, Riggio, Haydel & Mordaunt has served the legal needs of a diverse clientele from its downtown Stockton offices. The attorneys of the firm have built a reputation for legal excellence combined with community achievement.

The firm has grown from two lawyers at its inception in 1972 to 20 lawyers in 1989.

Diehl, Steinheimer, Riggio, Haydel & Mordaunt was founded by Joseph W. Diehl, who had been practicing law in a Stockton firm since his 1950 graduation from Boalt Hall School of Law at the University of California, Berkeley. The history of the firm reflects Diehl's primary objective—to create a law office that maximizes efficient and comprehensive service to clients while functioning productively in a congenial atmosphere.

The firm maintains a commitment to the vitality of downtown Stockton. It represents major downtown property owners, businesses, and developers of redevelopment properties. Attorneys serve on the board of directors and committees of the Stockton Chamber of Commerce and are active in downtown business groups. The firm's offices have always been located just a few steps from the San Joaquin County Courthouse. The practice began in the Bank of America Building at the corner of San Joaquin and Main streets. The firm moved into the downtown landmark San Joaquin First Federal Savings and Loan Plaza next to the courthouse in 1976.

The firm maintains a diverse civil practice. A substantial portion of the practice consists of civil litigation at both the trial and appellate levels. Long known for its expertise in defending claims of negligence against professionals in health care, architecture and engineering, law, accounting, and real estate fields, the firm also applies its expertise to litigation of business and commercial disputes, business torts, claims against public entities, and all types of personal injury and property damage actions. It maintains a strong insurance law practice as well.

Clients also rely upon the firm's ability to develop and maintain new business entities and analyze and implement matters of business, estate, and tax planning.

The firm has extensive experience in representing public entities in central California, including special districts, community college, and K-12 school districts, and county government departments.

The firm's practice is regional in scope—attorneys routinely appear in the courts of the five-county central valley and mountain area that includes San Joaquin (Stockton), Stanislaus (Modesto), Amador (Jackson), Calaveras (San Andreas), and Tuolumne (Sonora) counties. The practice also extends north throughout the Central Valley, west to the Bay Area, south to the Fresno-Visalia area, and east over the Sierras to Mono and Inyo counties and throughout Nevada. The firm opened a Sonora office in the fall of 1989.

Clients of Diehl, Steinheimer, Riggio, Haydel & Mordaunt benefit from the firm's decision to keep pace with rapid technological advances. The keys to successfully managing today's complex litigation are

From left: Keith Soressi, Max Steinheimer, Kate Segerstrom, Robert Werth, William Fulbright, and Donald Riggio.

cost control and developing the best-possible position early in the lawsuit. The firm is a leader in the use of litigation paralegals to reduce costs and assist in the rapid analysis of documents and issues. Both attorneys and paralegals use specialized data-base and text search and retrieval computer programs to manage cases that frequently involve tens of thousands of documents and hundreds of witnesses. The firm's extensive in-house library includes computerized legal research and access to worldwide data bases covering thousands of technical subjects. The library's computers also provide access to business information services, keeping clients informed on financial and regulatory matters.

The firm has developed expertise in utilizing mediation to resolve construction litigation cases involving building failures, a particularly troublesome and expensive type of lawsuit. Utilizing these methods the firm has handled major lawsuits arising out of such diverse events as delta levee failures, groundwater contamination in the South San Joaquin County area, sewer and industrial plant design failures in Nevada and California, and the catastrophic wildfires of the Monterey Peninsula.

The expertise Diehl, Steinheimer, Riggio, Haydel & Mordaunt offers to its clients is echoed by the contributions of the attorneys to professional and community organizations. Firm members have served as president and members of the board of governors and chairmen of committees and sections of the San Joaquin County Bar Association.

The firm's attorneys are regularly appointed as arbitrators in judicial-ordered arbitration proceedings and serve as judges pro tem by appointment of the county's judges. The firm donates legal services to local charitable and service organizations.

From left to right are Peter Kelly, William Johnson, Kevin Seibert, Joseph Fagundes, and Gary Cassel.

Members of the firm belong to the specialty bar associations, and are active in the Association of Defense Counsel of Northern California and Nevada. A principal in the firm serves as a director of the association. Attorneys of the firm have been elected to membership in the prestigious American Board of Trial Advocates and the California Medical-Legal Committee, a medical malpractice defense lawyer association.

The firm's philosophy encourages public service in nonlegal areas. The attorneys devote their time and expertise to civic groups, youth sports, service clubs, churches, university fund raising, and other charitable organizations. Several members of the firm contribute their time as coaches and committee chairmen of youth sports teams and programs, including soccer, basketball, softball, and baseball.

A principal in the firm has served for more than 10 years as a trustee of the Lincoln Unified School District, including four terms as board president. Attorneys serve on the Lodi Unified School District Budget and student housing committees. Members of the firm also belong to traditional service clubs, hold leadership positions in local church communities, and devote time to university alumni and athletic affairs.

Utilizing the best of modern technology and legal tools and maintaining a clear view of the needs of the Central Valley region, Diehl, Steinheimer, Riggio, Haydel & Mordaunt is ready to move forward and keep pace with the exciting, explosive growth that Stockton and San Joaquin County will experience in the next decade.

From left: Karen Denise Lee, Joseph Diehl, Scott Malm, and Douglas Haydel.

Feldman, Waldman & Kline

The attorneys of Feldman, Waldman & Kline serve a broad base of Stockton clients from the stately 100-year-old Sperry Building. The historic building, at 146 West Weber Avenue, is designated as a federal, state, and local landmark.

Providing the highest-possible quality of legal services to the Stockton community and its surrounding communities is an integral part of the philosophy of Feldman, Waldman & Kline. Just as important is the firm's commitment to meeting the needs of both large organizations and individual clients at a fair and reasonable cost.

To meet these goals the Stockton firm of Zuckerman & Hartmann merged with the San Francisco law firm of Feldman, Waldman & Kline in 1985. After interviewing a number of San Francisco law firms, Feldman, Waldman & Kline was selected as best suited to the specialized needs of the Stockton firm and its varied clients. The merger, designed to meet the complex business and litigation needs of the Stockton firm's growing number of clients, has provided the resources needed to fully service the community.

The objective of Feldman, Waldman & Kline is to grow with the community while continuing to provide a broad range of cost-effective legal services utilizing the firm's staff of 48 attorneys. The firm's offices are linked by state-of-the-art telecommunication methods, allowing rapid drafting and transfer of legal documents no matter where the lawyer and client are located. The result has been to provide the specialties and services of a San Francisco law firm to Stockton clients while retaining a strong local presence.

The Stockton office includes attorneys George Hartmann, Gerald Sherwin, and Martha Shaver. Feldman, Waldman & Kline's office in Stockton, located at 146 West Weber Avenue, is a federal, state, and local historic landmark. The building, constructed in 1888, was formerly used as a paymaster's office by the Sperry Flour Mill Company. The structure was restored more than five years ago.

Feldman, Waldman & Kline's specialties include real estate development, acquisition, disposition, syndication, and land-use planning. The firm also specializes in lender representation, with an emphasis on secured lending and real estate-related matters, and complex litigation matters, including business and bankruptcy, lending practices, class actions, condemnation, and general commercial litigation. Feldman, Waldman & Kline also offers expertise in corporate transactions, taxation and tax litigation, federal and state security laws, labor and employee relations, creditor/debtor remedies, estate planning, and bankruptcy.

Grant Thornton

Grant Thornton has established itself as accountant and management consultant to a diverse array of prominent local businesses.

Dedicated to serving its many clients, the Stockton office of Grant Thornton is a professional, full-service public accounting firm with expertise in audit, tax, consulting, and accounting.

While Grant Thornton is international in scope, Grant Thornton locally is very much rooted in Stockton, having evolved from several companies going back to Lyman and Keister and its founding at the end of World War I.

The Stockton office is located on the third floor of the Waterfront Towers at 509 West Weber Avenue and serves more than 2,000 clients ranging from individuals to major corporations. The local office is headed by six partners and four managers and includes roughly 55 employees, representing expertise in audit, tax, consulting, and accounting services.

Grant Thornton's philosophy is that the quality of service that professionals provide is as important as the work they perform. It is a belief reflected in the service standards established by the company.

In striving for excellence, Grant Thornton maintains a ratio of partners to staff that is among the lowest of all major firms. That assures that each client receives the same level of close, professional attention. Grant Thornton recruits, trains, and promotes people with outstanding technical skills who understand the meaning of providing superior service to clients.

Nationally, Grant Thornton is one of the world's largest certified public accounting firms. Founded in 1924, the company has more than 50 offices located in major commercial centers throughout the United States. Grant Thornton also is represented in 150 cities abroad through Grant Thornton International.

The firm employs 2,800 professionals, including 700 partners, principals, and managers. This enables the company to maintain a personal relationship with clients, while providing a broad range of technical expertise and in-depth industry experience available only from a major, national firm.

As with all of the offices of the firm, the Stockton operation benefits from the support of Grant Thornton's national office in Chicago. The resources provided enable each office to maintain the highest level of professional expertise and to coordinate engagements among offices where specialists are required.

Grant Thornton also participates in professional associations, including state-certified public accounting societies, senior committees of the American Institute of Certified Public Accountants, and task forces of the Financial Accounting Standards Board.

Photo by Kerrick James

Photo by Steve Pereira

Chapter 9

Building Greater Stockton

From concept to completion, real estate professionals and construction companies shape the Stockton of tomorrow.

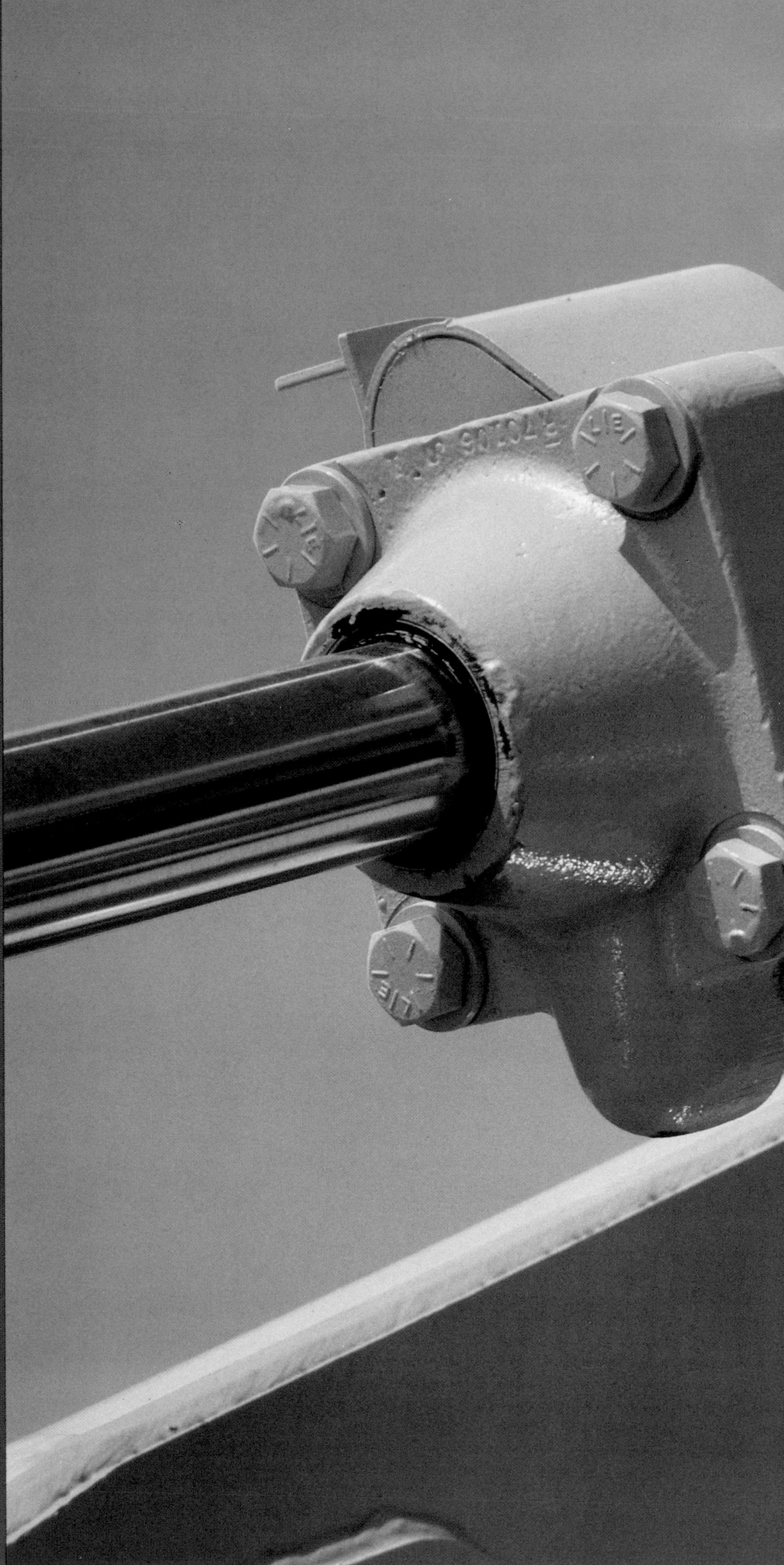

Photo by Mark Gibson

A. G. Spanos Construction, Inc.; 148

*Beck Development Co., Inc.
Beck Construction Company
Beck and Ratto Realtors, Inc.; 152*

The Grupe Company; 154

Teichert Construction; 156

McMasters & Westland; 157

A.G. Spanos Construction, Inc.

The founder and chairman of nine companies that bear his name, Alex G. Spanos is recognized as one of the most dynamic entrepreneurs in today's business world. Yet, for all his far-flung interests, Spanos has continued to call Stockton his home, while contributing greatly to its commercial and cultural success.

His latest proposal is the A.G. Spanos Park, a self-contained community that will consist of 7,200 dwelling units. The project is valued at one billion dollars, and, when completed, will be located north of Bear Creek roughly five miles from downtown Stockton on Interstate 5. Spanos Park will encompass 1,300 acres both east and west of the freeway with a magnificent view of Mount Diablo and the majestic San Joaquin Delta. It will feature residential neighborhoods designed to meet the needs of every life-style, from young families to senior citizens. The plan will include three major lakes, a planned business park with lake frontage, retail centers, four landscaped public parks, a delta-access 200-slip marina, a four-baseball-diamond and eight-soccer-field sports park, four public school sites, landscaped common areas, and lushly landscaped road islands and parkways.

Spanos' plans for Stockton are no less than those that the past 30 years have seen him almost single-handedly build—a construction empire spanning 15 states and making the Spanos corporation one of the top building giants in America.

ABOVE: Alex and Faye Spanos

LEFT: As a result of his purchase of the San Diego Chargers, Alex Spanos became aware of the development opportunities in the team's home city. A.G. Spanos Construction, Inc., developed the Mission Hills project there in 1986.

In the past 15 years A.G. Spanos Construction has emerged from a small-town operation to a company now ranking among the top 10 in the nation in apartment housing. The next five-year cycle will find Spanos Construction back in commercial building, with plans to expand in the residential apartment market. Having conducted almost $3 billion in business during the past five years alone, the company is projected to exceed that amount over the next five-year cycle.

Under the guidance of Alex Spanos, his companies have diversified into new business ventures. Initial involvement in syndication has flourished to surpass expectations, and future plans call for the development of the AGS Financial Corporation into a full-service syndication

Alex Spanos with sons Michael (seated) and Dean, and son-in-law Barry L. Ruhl (right).

and financial services firm.

Today Alex Spanos' far-reaching empire includes A.G. Spanos Construction, Inc.; A.G. Spanos Development, Inc.; A.G. Spanos Enterprises, Inc.; A.G. Spanos Management, Inc.; AGS Financial Corp.; A.G. Spanos Jet Center; A.G. Spanos Properties, Inc.; A.G. Spanos Realty, Inc.; AGS Securities Corp.; and A.G. Spanos Land Company.

The A.G. Spanos Jet Center grew out of a need to satisfy a demanding travel schedule for company executives. The most modern private facility of its kind in Northern California, it consists of a 38-foot-high all-purpose hangar, with 40,000 square feet of floor space, including an office building. The jet center accommodates private aircraft from throughout the United States and offers services that include sales, rentals, propeller and plane repair, and maintenance.

The corporate officers, in addition to Spanos, who is chairman of the board and chief executive officer, are his sons, Dean A. and Michael A. Spanos, and son-in-law, Dr. Barry Ruhl.

A fierce competitor, Spanos has pursued his goals with unflagging enthusiasm, setting personal and business records annually. One of those goals was realized in 1984, when Spanos purchased the San Diego Chargers of the National Football League.

The story of Alex G. Spanos is one of hard work, dedication, and faith. He was born in Stockton on September 28, 1923, to Gus and Eva Spanos and attended local schools before going on to California Polytechnic State University in San Luis Obispo and the University of the Pacific in Stockton. He later served a stint in the U.S. Air Force and was honorably discharged in February 1946. Two years later, on August 22, 1948, he and the former Faye Faklis were married. In later years Spanos was to say of his wife, "The most important influence in my life is my wife. Her unfaltering support and love have given me the peace of mind that is so essential to my total success."

Spanos started his working career employed at his father's bakery. After he quit, he struck out on his own and, with an $800 loan from a local bank, he bought a panel truck and set himself up in business as the sole proprietor of the A.G. Spanos Catering Co. During the next few years Spanos worked 16 hours per day supplying meals to hundreds of Central Valley farm workers.

Spanos used the money he saved to invest in real estate properties that soon began to pay off handsomely. His success led him to take an even bigger step against the advice of many friends and associates. In 1960 he formed his own construction company. In the years that followed, he erected a small number of commercial buildings and apartments in the Stockton area; his continued success led him eventually to

Alex Spanos' dreams for his home city are epitomized in Spanos Park, a master-planned community that, when completed, will feature housing to fit different life-styles, schools, a lakefront business park, four landscaped parks, three major lakes, and a marina with delta access.

A.G. Spanos Development, Inc., has been active in growing metropolitan areas nationwide, such as Atlanta, Georgia. The firm's residential developments in that city include Le Parc (top left) and Chelsea Park (above) and (left).

further expand.

Although Alex Spanos heads the companies that bear his name, decisions are made jointly by Spanos and his sons and son-in-law. Together they are the driving force behind each business venture. "Our projects are tops because we take the time to see that quality, aesthetics, and function blend together," Spanos explains. "We build with one goal in mind—to be the best at what we do."

Dean A. Spanos is Alex Spanos' eldest son and closest adviser. As president and chief executive officer of the Spanos corporate organization, Dean Spanos is responsible for all construction operations nationwide, as well as all financial matters relating to acquisition and development. He has directed the construction of more than 21,000 apartment units and 650,000 square feet of office space since joining the company in 1972. He also is vice-chairman of the San Diego Chargers and as such represents that organization at National Football League meetings.

Barry Ruhl is executive vice-president of A.G. Spanos Construction, Inc., A.G. Spanos Management, Inc., and A.G. Spanos Development, Inc. He has a variety of responsibilities that include managing the divisions and all construction projects in Georgia, Texas, and Washington. That includes the construction of 4,700 apartment units in Texas—2,016 in Irving, 250 in Arlington, and 1,240 in Fort Worth.

Michael Spanos, the youngest member of the Spanos executives, is executive vice-president of A.G. Spanos Construction, Inc., A.G. Spanos Management, Inc., and A.G. Spanos Development, Inc. Michael Spanos has completed three major apartment complexes and is responsible for the construction of more than 2,400 apartment units.

Alex Spanos, however, takes a

Among Alex Spanos' philanthropic gifts to the Stockton community was the renovation of the 1,000-seat conservatory building at UOP. In 1987 it was renamed the Faye Spanos Concert Hall, in honor of the developer's wife.

hands-on approach to everything that relates to his business. He is untiring in his commitment to excel in all business endeavors. Traveling more than 4,000 miles per week to oversee his construction projects, explore new investment opportunities, and confer with San Diego Chargers personnel, Spanos is the embodiment of a man on the move.

Yet for all of his business expertise, Alex Spanos still manages to find time to help others. A noted philanthropist, he has donated millions of dollars to benefit numerous charities, educational institutions, hospitals, churches, civic organizations, and athletic associations.

Major recipients of his generosity include the Children's Hospital of San Francisco, the Eisenhower Medical Center, Dameron Hospital of Stockton, St. Joseph's Hospital of Stockton, the Betty Ford Center, the Children's Hospital of San Diego, the Graduate Theological Union of the University of California, and earthquake victims in Greece.

For the past 25 years Alex Spanos has also given his full support to the University of the Pacific. His latest contribution was a sizable financial gift to totally renovate the school's 1,000-seat conservatory building, which in May of 1987 was reopened as the Faye Spanos Concert Hall.

Comedian Bob Hope has said of his friend, "Without a doubt, Alex Spanos is one of the most successful and charitable individuals I know."

Barron Hilton, chairman of the Hilton Hotel Corporation, stated, "Alex is one of America's great businessmen. I know him as a dedicated family man as well as a sportsman and trusted friend."

Jerry Reinsdorf, a partner in Bojer Financial, Limited, says, "Alex Spanos is the only person I know with whom I can make a multimillion-dollar deal on a handshake. In every instance, Alex' word is his bond."

Spanos is a trustee of the Eisenhower Medical Center, a governor of the Ronald Reagan Presidential Foundation, an honorary regent of the University of the Pacific and the American College in Greece, a past trustee of the Fine Arts Museum of San Francisco and the Children's Hospital of San Francisco, and a past governor of the United Services Organization.

In recognition of his business and philanthropic activities, Spanos has received many honors and awards, including the Statue of Liberty-Ellis Island Medal of Honor, the Horatio Alger Award, and AHEPA's Aristotelian Award.

Local recognition has come often over the years. In 1972 Spanos was presented with a citation from the Stockton Parks and Recreation Commission for his outstanding community service, and in 1980 he received the Stocktonian of the Year Award presented by the Stockton Realty Board. In 1987 he was inducted into the Stockton Business Hall of Fame, and that same year he was given the Distinguished Good Citizen Award by the Forty Niner Council of the Boy Scouts of America at its annual dinner.

Nor has his wife been without recognition. In 1971 the new facility at the Trinity School for Children in Ukiah was named the Faye A. Spanos Residence for Girls in her honor. And in 1973 the Alex and Faye Spanos Distinguished Teaching Award was established at the University of the Pacific by the Spanos children to honor their parents on their 25th wedding anniversary.

Alex Spanos' personal life has been as rewarding and fulfilling as his extraordinary career. Alex and Faye Spanos have created an environment of warmth and solidarity for their family, which includes two sons and two daughters, a son-in-law, a daughter-in-law, and seven grandchildren.

Beck Development Co., Inc. Beck Construction Company Beck and Ratto Realtors, Inc.

Beck Development Co., Inc., of Stockton is a highly respected and well-known name in California, noted for its quality-conscious, well-detailed, and aesthetically pleasing homes.

The company was founded in 1965 as a family venture. Lonnie Beck, one of the founders and a contractor himself, began his business career by building and selling his houses. Since its establishment as a force in the building industry, Beck Development Co., Inc., has built an estimated 6,000 homes in Stockton.

In fact, when driving around Stockton, it is difficult to miss the many beautiful homes that Beck Development Co., Inc., has built over the years—homes that company officials believe will continue to serve generation after generation of home owners.

Over the years and currently, Beck Development Co., Inc., has built, and is building and developing, attractive new subdivisions in Dublin, Manteca, Elk Grove, Stockton, San Diego, and Vallejo. The combined resources of the land acquisition, development, and sales divisions are working toward the firm's goal of producing 600 to 700 houses per year throughout Northern and Southern California.

The company's overriding philosophy is to build spacious homes at reasonable prices while keeping the quality for which its name has become synonymous throughout the industry. The houses, which vary in style, range in size from 1,500 to 2,800 square feet and contain from three to five bedrooms. Designed for family-oriented living, the homes generally appeal to middle-income families, although prices vary according to location. According to company officials, its homes in Southern California will sell for between $250,000 and $400,000, while in Dublin, they are reselling in the $200,000 to $275,000 range. In Stockton, Manteca, and Elk Grove, the prices range from $122,500 to $170,000.

Because company officials must often fly to meetings elsewhere in California, the firm owns a Beech King Air twin turboprop airplane.

Corporate headquarters is situated at 3114 West Hammer Lane, just east of the Interstate 5 interchange. The tastefully decorated two-story office building features an executive lounge, a racquetball

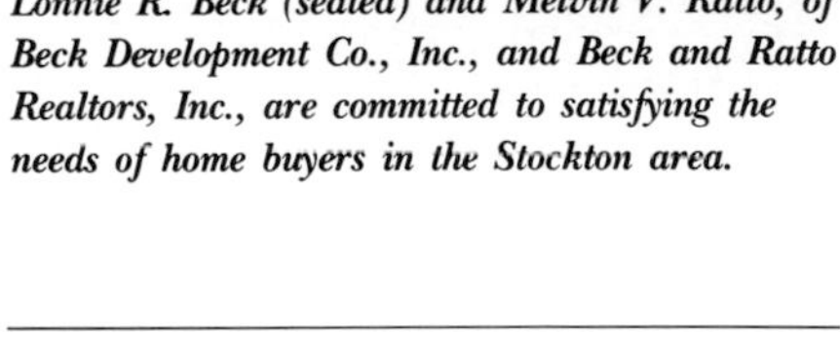

Lonnie R. Beck (seated) and Melvin V. Ratto, of Beck Development Co., Inc., and Beck and Ratto Realtors, Inc., are committed to satisfying the needs of home buyers in the Stockton area.

Beck Development Co. Inc., completed this 72-unit condominium complex on Kelley Drive in Stockton. Opened in 1985, the complex is now 100-percent occupied.

court, a steam room and spa, and a putting green, where employees can relax during breaks. The company currently employs 40 people in its development, construction, sales, and commercial/residential income property divisions. The executive offices are used as a busy contact center for an array of projects that include Beck Development Co. Inc. and Beck Construction Company.

Beck Development Co., Inc.'s, activities include the design, construction, and community concept planning of the developments, while Beck Construction Company is responsible for building and managing, for its own account, a number of multiple-dwelling communities and business properties.

Overseeing the apartments is the responsibility of Beck Construction Company's Property Management Department, a task that requires supervision of hundreds of rental units, including duplexes, triplexes, fourplexes, town houses, and condominiums in the Stockton area. All units are well maintained and managed by on-site residential managers who can boast an enviable vacancy rate of generally less than one-half of one percent.

Beck and Ratto Realtors, Inc., relocated to this spacious new headquarters on Kelley Drive in the spring of 1987.

The Property Management Department also leases, manages, and maintains the Colonial Plaza Shopping Center, which consists of individual shops, a Fry's Food and Drug Store, and three land pads occupied by a Fosters Freeze, a Der Wienerschnitzel, and a branch of the Sacramento Savings and Loan Association.

Beck Development Co., Inc., believes there is a need for new homes, not only in Northern California, but throughout the state, and that the need will continue to grow along with the population. The company offers standard amenities in each of its homes and, depending on the locations, will provide custom upgrades to the amenities offered.

Across the street from the corporate headquarters are the beautiful new offices of Beck and Ratto Realtors, Inc., a company that was formed more than six years ago by Mel Ratto and Lonnie Beck as a culmination to a dream to further satisfy the needs of the home-buying public through a home resale organization. Started with just one agent, the firm now has a staff of some 14 professionals who actively market properties in Stockton and surrounding cities. It is estimated, however, that 50 percent of the company's sales are for people who are moving up to a new Beck Development Co., Inc., home.

The skilled staff employed by the firm has received some of the most prestigious and coveted awards presented by the local board of realtors, including the Master Club, recently awarded to five of the Beck and Ratto agents.

As stated, Beck Development Co., Inc., Beck Construction Company, and Beck and Ratto Realtors, Inc., are companies whose traditions and management philosophies ensure quality residential units for the communities and the people they serve.

One of Beck Development Co., Inc.'s, recent projects is the Country Greens subdivision in Stockton.

The Grupe Company

ABOVE: The Country Fair at Brookside in Stockton is The Grupe Company's major fund raiser. Since 1981 the event has generated one million dollars for the benefit of various charities.

ABOVE LEFT and LEFT: Many of Grupe's developments feature lakeside living, which is conducive to a wide range of water-oriented recreational activities.

BELOW: Fountains enhance Grupe communities with a soothing ambience.

The Grupe Company is a diversified real estate development, management, and equities firm based in Stockton. Known as a "planner for the future" and "an architect of lifestyle," the company began in 1966, and its Lincoln Village West soon became known as an innovative master-planned community that pleasantly and conveniently integrated commercial and residential development with recreational amenities centered around a man-made lake. Subsequently four additional lake communities have been built in Stockton: North Lake, Quail Lake, Meadow Lake, and The Landing.

Today The Grupe Company is one of the largest privately held real estate development firms in the United States, with 50 communities located in eight states. These communities house more than 30,000 residents and include one million square feet of office space, having a current market value in excess of $1.5 billion. In all developments Grupe has continued its coordinated planning and has most often incorporated lakes, waterways, and plush landscaping; the company has captured numerous awards of excellence for its creative plans and attention to interior and exterior detail.

In addition, The Grupe Company has consistently maintained a commitment of quality service to its clients, and has become both an economic and social contributor to its communities. More than one mil-

lion dollars has been raised for charity since the inception of the biennial fund raiser, the Country Fair.

Chairman and chief executive officer Greenlaw "Fritz" Grupe, Jr., comments, "It has been a pleasure to make an impact on the quality of life available to the people of Stockton and the other communities in which the company has developed. I look forward to continuing that commitment in the years ahead."

TOP RIGHT: Dining at the waterfront provides a relaxing experience.

ABOVE: Lincoln Village West is typical of The Grupe Company's quality Stockton developments.

Teichert Construction

In Stockton, when you think of construction, you think of Teichert. For almost a half-century Teichert's steady growth and expansion has paralleled that of the city of Stockton. Demonstrating the firm's expertise in both the public and private sectors, the many area projects bearing the Teichert name range from the Stockton Airport, built during World War II, to a 200-acre master-planned community now under development in Stockton.

Teichert Construction has been active in Stockton longer than any other general engineering contractor. The firm is a reliable, community-minded company, well known for its dual commitment to innovative technology and traditional values.

The practice of utilizing all available technological advances enables the firm to consistently complete projects on or ahead of schedule—performance that produces significant cost savings and increased profits for customers.

At the same time, the firm's ongoing commitment to traditional values is evident in the people of Teichert and in the high quality of the product and service they provide to Teichert customers.

The firm has a proud heritage. Founded in Sacramento in 1887, A. Teichert & Son holds California Contractors License No. 8, the oldest active license in the state.

Over the years Teichert has grown from a one-man business to a corporation with more than 1,400 employees that does more than $250 million worth of business a year throughout the North State. Its operations today encompass Teichert Construction, with offices in Sacramento, Stockton, and Woodland; Teichert Aggregates, which operates 11 aggregate and ready-mix sites; the Teichert Land Company, which manages and develops land owned by the corporation; and the Mobile Equipment Division, which supplies equipment to the construction and aggregate operations.

MISSION STATEMENT

The *principles* listed here are excerpted from the comprehensive Mission Statement that guides the day-to-day operations of Teichert Construction.

Quality: To achieve customer satisfaction, the quality of our services must be a top priority.

Customers: We are committed to contributing to the success of our customers. This is the basis of our relationship with them.

Improvement: Continuous improvement is essential to our success. We must strive for excellence in everything we do.

Employees: Employee involvement is our way of life. We are a team. We must treat each other with trust and respect.

Affirmative Action: We welcome men and women alike without regard to their ethnic origin or personal beliefs.

Safety: Safety comes first. The safety of our employees, our customers, and the general public is essential to our business.

Integrity: Our integrity will never be compromised. Our company goals must be pursued in a socially responsible manner, commanding respect and contributing positively to society and our environment.

McMasters & Westland

In the past two years the Central Valley Division of McMasters & Westland in Stockton has leased more than 3 million square feet of warehouse and manufacturing space, sold more than 1.8 million square feet of commercial and industrial buildings, and brokered 553 acres of land in the Stockton, Modesto, and Tracy areas. The total value of those transactions exceeded $50 million, accounting for more than half of the commercial brokerage activity in the area.

All of that business did not happen by chance. It has taken a great deal of effort and faith on the part of the McMasters & Westland staff, which is headed by Ernest J. Pearson, managing partner of the Central Valley Division.

As Pearson sees it, the potential in Stockton continues to be the abundance of inexpensive land, excellent transportation, low-cost housing, and a surplus of trainable moderately priced labor.

Stockton is not a bedroom community, but a self-contained metropolitan area with its own recreation, arts, and culture; people do not have to look outward from Stockton to live a complete life-style, according to Pearson.

McMasters & Westland's staff includes (from left): John Pedri, Lani McMahan, Tom Davis, Laura Hidalgo, Hal Richardson, and managing partner Ernest Pearson.

Pearson, who has been in the business 20 years, originally worked for Coldwell Banker and served as vice-president and branch manager for Cushman & Wakefield in the Bay Area. In 1982 Pearson moved to the Central Valley and started his own company, Delta Pacific Realty Corp., which specialized in industrial sales and leasing. In 1984 Pearson sold the firm to McMasters & Westland. In return, he took a partnership interest in the larger company.

McMasters & Westland has been in business since 1977 and was founded in Walnut Creek. It dominates the office leasing business in the East Bay. Recently McMasters & Westland was merged with TRI of San Francisco. The merger has resulted in an increased capability in Northern California, comprising more than 200 commercial agents.

Pearson, who originally saw an opportunity in the early 1980s to move into the valley and specialize, believes McMasters & Westland has been enormously successful in terms of encouraging developers from the Bay Area to locate in the Stockton area and acquire land and buildings, which the Central Valley Division then represents and leases to tenants. It has been a matter of opening Stockton up to a greater range of activities, investors, and developers, according to Pearson.

McMasters & Westland employs six salespeople in its Stockton operation, concentrating on Stockton, Modesto, and Tracy. The company is located in a 2,000-square-foot office at 188 Frank West Circle in the Grupe Business Park in Stockton and maintains a satellite office in Modesto.

This 750,000-square-foot distribution center is represented by McMasters & Westland for Lincoln Property Company.

Chapter **10**

Quality of Life

Medical and educational institutions contribute to the quality of life of Stockton residents.

Photo by Mark Gibson

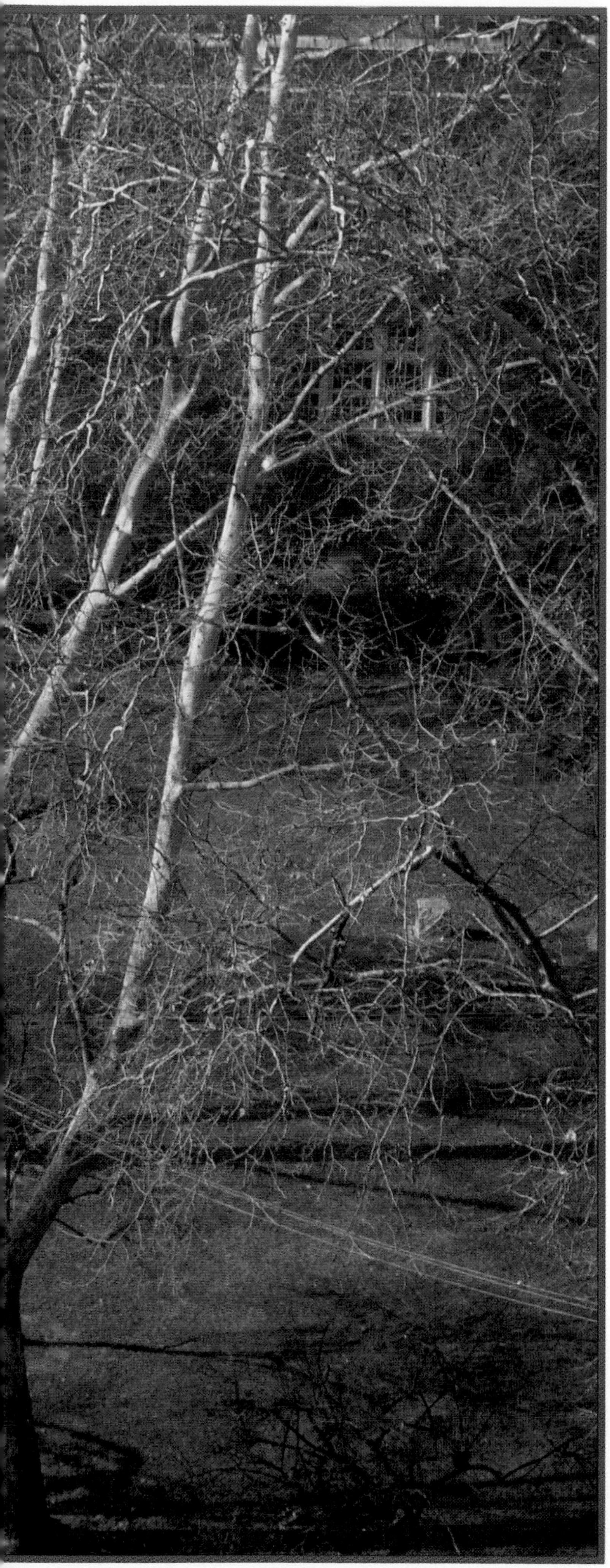

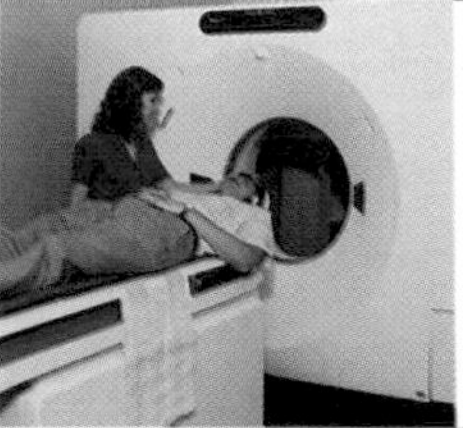

S.J. MAGNETIC RESONANCE CENTER

St. Joseph's Medical Center of Stockton

St. Joseph's Medical Center of Stockton—Where Quality is Tradition—serves the northern San Joaquin Valley as an acute care medical facility specializing in cancer, heart, respiratory, and emergency cases. A service of St. Joseph's HealthCare Corporation, the steadily growing 321-bed medical center, conveniently located at 1800 North California Street, attends to 14,000 inpatients and 300,000 outpatient contacts per year.

The breadth of programs and services St. Joseph's offers to the community can be attributed to the founding principles established by Father William O'Connor whose dream of care for the needy became St. Joseph's.

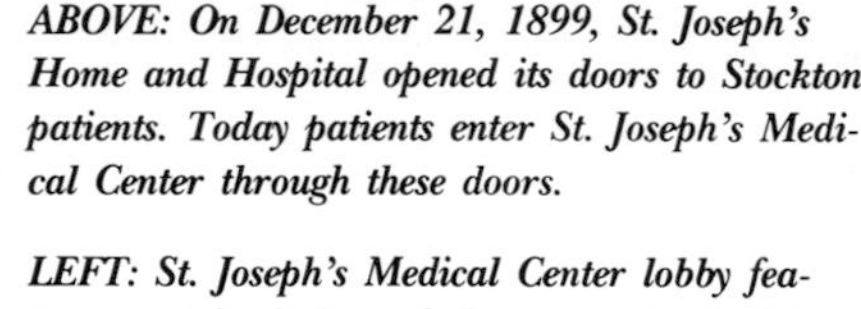

ABOVE: On December 21, 1899, St. Joseph's Home and Hospital opened its doors to Stockton patients. Today patients enter St. Joseph's Medical Center through these doors.

LEFT: St. Joseph's Medical Center lobby features a stained-glass window created especially for the hospital by internationally renowned artist Diana Schor.

St. Joseph's was built with the enthusiastic support of the community. For years citizens had wanted a premier health care institution to meet their ever-increasing needs. On March 19, 1899, the Feast Day of St. Joseph, the cornerstone was laid. During the ceremonies the Most Reverend P.W. Riordan, Archbishop of the Diocese, noted:

How glad the people of Stockton seem . . . This great work . . . is a great charity to the care and generosity of the . . . people of this town. In the land in which we live, the mountains contain the water; there the snows fall; there the rivers rise; and from these the fountains come. They come down on these lowlands and make them fertile, and bring riches with them. And so it should be with the people. There are some who store the goods of this world, and they should open their reservoirs of wealth and pour them down on those who have none. Almighty God gives this chance to those who have. . . This home is to be open to all classes of people, irrespective of race, nationality, or creed, for charity knows no creed; knows no race. It is the one thing that binds us together.

On December 21, 1899, St. Joseph's Home and Hospital opened its doors to residents and patients.

It takes forward thinking to develop and maintain the reputation for quality that St. Joseph's enjoys. That reputation is built upon an ever-increasing number of touchstones to excellence, including introducing the use of the wonder drug penicillin to the area; establishing one of Northern California's first radiation therapy departments; installing the area's first cardioscope; implanting the area's first nuclear-powered pacemaker; performing the county's first open-heart surgery; opening the county's first Crisis Intervention Unit; installing the area's first CAT Scanner; providing CareVan, a mobile health care service for the needy; having the only multidisciplinary Pulmonary Rehabilitation Program between Sacramento and Fresno; establishing the region's first hospital-based Fitness Center for community members; and the list continues.

The medical staff play an important role in patient care at St. Joseph's. Nearly 400 physicians, 70 percent of whom are board certified, practice 44 specialties at the medical center. Physicians serve on 50

ABOVE: The 1916 entrance to St. Joseph's Hospital.

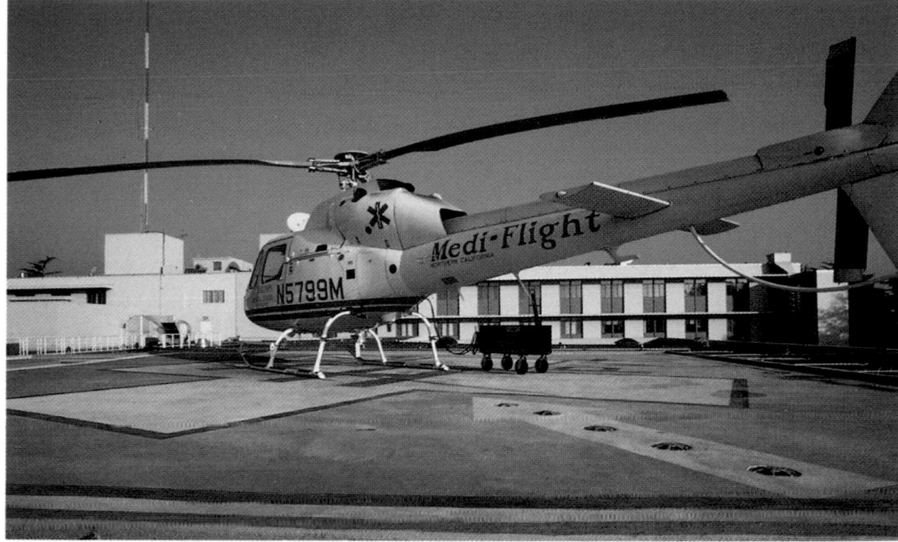

RIGHT: St. Joseph's MEDI-FLIGHT, a regional air-medical transport service, features a jet helicopter outfitted with the latest in emergency care equipment.

committees, most of which evaluate and monitor patient care. They examine resources and the use of those resources to ensure their proper utilization. They also review new medical devices to determine the appropriateness of their use and monitor the use of drugs, tests, and new equipment. The medical staff at St. Joseph's works to assure every patient receives quality care.

Today the institution that O'Connor and the people of Stockton worked so hard to build has become a dynamic, full-service, medical/surgical/intensive care health organization serving not only Stockton but all of San Joaquin County, the foothills of the Sierra, and the delta country.

St. Joseph's Medical Center offers the community sophisticated programs ranging from cardiac rehabilitation, chemical dependency, psychiatric medicine, and diagnostic imaging to nuclear medicine; radiation therapy; outpatient surgery; nutrition counseling; physical, occupational, and speech therapies; maternity services; sports medicine; pulmonary rehabilitation; lithotripsy; hyperbaric oxygen therapy; Optifast weight management; and diabetes management. In addition, St. Joseph's owns and operates HealthCare Clinical Laboratory (with eight drawing stations conveniently located around the city of Stockton with courier service to and from other communities), Home Health Care, Home Support Services, a Learning Center, and the area's first hospital-based distinct part/skilled nursing facility. There are other services as well. St. Joseph's is dedicated to meeting the needs of the people it serves.

St. Joseph's HealthCare Corporation, activated in 1986, assures the region of a continuum of health care through a carefully studied program of diversification. In addition to the medical center, St. Joseph's also operates Abbey Medical; Parkside Recovery, with psychiatric and chemical dependency programs; OMNI Health Plan, a hospital- and physician-owned Health Maintenance Organization; Mark Twain St. Joseph's Hospital in San Andreas; O'Connor Woods—a retirement community; and two immediate care facilities—one on March Lane in Stockton and the other on Louise Avenue in Manteca. St. Joseph's has mobilized its numerous resources to make them conveniently available for area residents.

St. Joseph's HealthCare Corporation, complex and dynamic, is also involved in joint ventures with physicians and other area health care facilities, an example of which is the San Joaquin Magnetic Resonance Imaging Center.

Another example is found in St. Joseph's and Memorial Hospital Association of Modesto's joint operation of MEDI-FLIGHT of Northern California, a regional emergency air-medical transport service using twin jet Aerospatiale helicopters outfitted with the latest technology for emergency care.

Complementing its high-tech capabilities is St. Joseph's personal approach to patient care. Patients sometimes need more than medical care. Often a smile or a bit of music helps. That is why, for example, St. Joseph's includes music therapy as a part of patient care. Music can distract from pain, loneliness, and even boredom. The staff at St. Joseph's strives to be friendly and respect patient needs.

St. Joseph's Medical Center of Stockton's story is one of public service, professional pride, and commitment to personalized patient care.

University of the Pacific

Founded in 1851, the University of the Pacific is the first institution of higher education chartered in California.

Yet it is the future that concerns UOP president Bill L. Atchley. The future, he said in his inaugural speech on April 16, 1988, lies with the university creating a new climate to nurture creativity and stimulate initiative.

Atchley said he wanted to create a climate where people have the freedom to make and learn from mistakes and where they know that innovation and effectiveness will be recognized and rewarded. "And it will be rewarded for performance in the classroom, in the laboratory, and in working with the public," said Atchley, in spelling out a six-point plan that celebrates UOP's past and builds on its future.

The beautiful facilities housing UOP's Conservatory of Music provide a perfect atmosphere for students preparing for the Bachelor of Music degree.

Atchley, who is the 22nd president to serve at UOP, forecast that the University of the Pacific will become known regionally and nationally as an institution that promises the uncommon educational experience.

Nationally UOP is widely regarded for its highly personalized and diverse educational experiences. With more than 100 majors offered through 11 schools and colleges, and programs in several foreign countries, the university enjoys an excellent reputation.

UOP is recognized as a pioneering and innovative institution. It established the first coeducational campus in the West, first university-affiliated Conservatory of Music, first medical school in Northern California (later it became a part of Stanford), and first four-year institution in the Central Valley. It also was first in the West to emphasize cooperative engineering programs, first to operate a School of Pharmacy on an 11-month basis, and first to send an entire class to an overseas campus.

The Robert E. Burns Tower, overlooking Knoles Lawn, is a recognized landmark for both the university and the Stockton community.

"Our goal," Atchley says, "is not to produce ivory-tower idealists or trained technological seals. Rather, the university's mission is to empower our students and nurture them so that when they leave our influence, they will be productive, creative, and useful citizens—and be leaders—in this nation and the world."

Statistics indicate that the students attending UOP are from 40 different states and 60 different countries, with out-of-state and foreign students accounting for 30 percent of the undergraduate student body.

Features of the Stockton campus include central administration, a liberal arts college, six professional schools, and a graduate school. The McGeorge School of Law, which joined with the university in 1966, is in Sacramento. The School of Dentistry in San Francisco, formerly the College of Physicians and Surgeons, became part of the university in 1962.

Schools at the Stockton campus are the College of the Pacific, which includes programs of liberal arts and science; the School of Education; Conservatory of Music; the School of Engineering; the School of Business and Public Administration; the School of International Stud-

The rose garden at Knoles Lawn is typical of the university's lush surroundings, conducive to the learning process.

ies; the School of Pharmacy; and University College, for adult reentry students.

The Stockton campus has 12 residence halls. There also are six fraternities and four sororities with houses along with university-owned apartment complexes. During the school year roughly 2,200 students reside on campus.

The coeducational student body enrollment numbers some 4,000 full-time students on the Stockton campus, 450 at the School of Dentistry, and 1,400 at the McGeorge School of Law.

As a major institution of higher learning, the university has a tremendous economic impact on Stockton, including $20.3 million awarded annually in financial aid, $3.5 million in research and training grants, $6 million in equipment and supplies purchases, and $30 million in annual expenditures in Stockton by the university, its students, and employees. The latter number roughly 975. The physical plant is valued in excess of $80 million, with more than $40 million invested in new construction since 1956.

Along with education, the University of the Pacific offers a broad range of entertainment and cultural events. The Drama Department stages a half-dozen major productions annually, as well as numerous one-act, improvisational, pantomime, and readers' theater programs. Fallon House Theater in Columbia State Park is the site of the drama department's summer repertory.

The Conservatory of Music provides a continuous series of programs with performances by faculty, students, and guest artists.

Lecturers and performers also visit the campus as guests of the Associated Students of the University, which also sponsors concerts. The university's radio station, KUOP-FM, broadcasts throughout the Central Valley.

In terms of athletics, UOP is a member of the Big West Conference. Male students compete in baseball, basketball, football, golf, swimming, tennis, and water polo; women compete in basketball, cross country, field hockey, softball, swimming, tennis, and volleyball. The women's volleyball team boasts two recent NCAA National Championships. There are also extensive intramural programs and physical education activity courses. Facilities include the 30,000-seat Amos Alonzo Stagg Memorial Stadium, the Alex G. Spanos Center, a gymnasium, tennis courts, and an Olympic-size swimming pool.

Founded by pioneer Methodist missionaries, the institution was moved in 1924 to Stockton from San Jose. The campus landscaping was guided by architect John McClaren, who designed San Francisco's Golden Gate Park. As anyone who has visited UOP can attest to, the Stockton campus is notable for its tall shade trees, redwood groves, and ivy-covered brick buildings surrounded by rich green lawns and flower gardens. The park-like setting in the heart of Stockton attracts many visitors, as well as conferences, special events, and summer programs. The campus often is used by Hollywood film producers as a location depicting an eastern Ivy League-type college.

Chartered as a university, the name was changed in the early 1900s to College of the Pacific and changed once more in the 1960s to the University of the Pacific. Many alumni, students, and parents describe UOP as "what a college should be."

The newly constructed Wm. Knox Holt Memorial Library is home to some 380,000 bound volumes, in addition to 360,000 periodicals and other media.

Stockton Radiology Medical Group, Inc.

LEFT: The staff of Stockton Radiology Medical Group, Inc., works closely with physicians to help them reach accurate diagnoses using radiological technology.

BELOW: Stockton Radiology's X-ray technologists pose in front of a General Electric Computed Tomography (CT) head and body scanner.

If one were looking for a single word to describe the close association between Stockton Radiology Medical Group, Inc., and the community, it might be "service." "We provide a service to the people and physicians in our community," explains Dr. Thomas A. Thomas, president of the group.

"Our contribution to the health care of the community is to assist the physician in making a correct diagnosis and to help him determine the extent of a disease or injury so he can provide the best treatment for his patient.

"The best treatment is based on an accurate diagnosis. We are here to help the physician care for his patients and to provide specialized radiological service for the community."

In an age of dramatic changes in medicine, Stockton Radiology Medical Group has been instrumental in bringing to Stockton new radiological technology and radiologists trained in the newest diagnostic techniques.

The doctors who make up Stockton Radiology are Thomas, Laszlo B. Fodor, M.D.; Javad Jamshidi, M.D.; Daniel W. Terry, Jr., M.D.; Jack L. Funamura, M.D; Louise Del-Paine, M.D.; and J. Kevin Mackey, M.D. Each is certified by the American Board of Radiology.

"The changes in radiological technology over the past 15 years have been immense," says Thomas, who is one of the seven doctors who make up Stockton Radiology. "The change is due primarily to Computed Tomography (CT), Magnetic Resonance Imaging (MRI), and interventional radiological techniques."

Stockton Radiology, along with St. Joseph's Medical Center, has pioneered the use in Stockton of Ultrasound, Nuclear Medicine, CT, MRI, and the development of interventional procedures, including vascular angioplasty. Ultrasound in particular has become a very useful tool, especially for examining pregnant women. Ultrasonography allows the doctors to actually see the infant and placenta inside the mother's womb and determine if any problems exist.

Some of the significant advances in medicine have been inconspicuous. Thomas notes, for example, that over a period of years there has been a substantial reduction, in some instances as much as 50 percent, in the amount of radiation exposure to the patient. This has been achieved, he says, mainly through refinements in techniques and equipment, development of high-speed screens and X-ray films, and low-radiation-dose isotopes. Ultrasound and Magnetic Resonance Imaging have furthur decreased exposure because radiation is not involved in these procedures.

Throughout its history Stockton Radiology has been closely associated with St. Joseph's Medical Center and provided professional diagnostic radiology and imaging services for inpatients and outpatients at the medical center.

In the 1950s the group pioneered in bringing high-voltage radiation therapy to the community, operating the first Cobalt Radiation Therapy Unit in conjunction with St. Joseph's Medical Center. As specialties became more complex and as the body of knowledge expanded, radiation therapy and diagnostic radiology separated. Individual specialists took over the radiation therapy aspect of radiology, and Stockton Radiology confined its work to diagnostic radiology.

***ABOVE:** The office staff at Stockton Radiology contributes to efficient operations and the commitment to service for which the group is known.*

***LEFT:** X-ray technologists Shelley Thompson and Rick Reed demonstrate the General Electric CT Scanner.*

Today Stockton Radiology is a referral group only. An individual cannot walk into Stockton Radiology and ask to have an X ray. "A person must have been referred to us by a physician, and, therefore, we work very closely with the physicians in our community," says Thomas.

Stockton Radiology Medical Group and its 18 employees occupy Suite 1A in the California Medical Center at 1617 North California Street, directly across from St. Joseph's Medical Center.

The group's history extends to the 1940s. The original radiologist was Dr. Edmund P. Halley, a descendant of the man who named Halley's Comet.

Thomas sees the future as a continuation of service to the people in the community. "Future radiological innovations and advances will be continually incorporated into our practice. We will recruit radiologists trained in the new modalities and bring them to the San Joaquin community as soon as possible." This is the "service" of Stockton Radiology Medical Group, Inc., to the people of its community.

San Joaquin Magnetic Resonance Imaging Center

For its aesthetic appeal, the building that houses San Joaquin Magnetic Resonance Center holds a design award from the City of Stockton.

The San Joaquin Magnetic Resonance Imaging Center, at 5375 North West Lane, is the first permanent magnetic resonance imaging site in San Joaquin County.

As such, it provides the community with a sense of pride. According to Dr. Javad Jamshidi, "Area residents are fortunate in having access to such an advanced medical technology in its early development."

Magnetic resonance imaging (MRI) is the most recent, sophisticated, and advanced imaging technique used in medicine. Unlike computed tomography (CT), which uses X rays, MRI is a product that combines a strong magnetic field, computers, and radio frequencies. It produces cross-section views of the body on different planes. These cross-section images provide excellent tissue contrast and anatomical details not available by any other imaging modality. In some instances, obtaining such information in the past required several days of hospitalization.

Bringing such advanced technology in its earliest stage to San Joaquin County required the teamwork and close cooperation between physicians, three radiology groups, and three hospitals. The result is the availability of a centralized and advanced medical imaging technology in San Joaquin County.

The computer age has dramatically changed the imaging technology in medicine. Eighty years after Roentgen's discovery of the X ray and its use in medicine, computed tomography revolutionized the imaging technology in the early 1970s. The early 1980s introduced magnetic resonance imaging.

Pioneers in utilizing the most advanced medical technology in their practice, the doctors of San Joaquin County felt it a necessity to have the developing technology of magnetic resonance imaging in their community in early 1985. Because of this cooperative effort, the San Joaquin Magnetic Resonance Center opened its door in September 1986. Since then it has expanded and acquired a second, more powerful magnet.

The superb anatomical details that can be seen on magnetic resonance images would provide the most accurate information to the doctors for diagnosing their patients' problems. Centralization of such an advanced technology not only made it available to the community much sooner but also helped to reduce the cost of its operation and, as a

LEFT and BELOW: The helpful staff at San Joaquin Magnetic Resonance Center assures a pleasant visit for MRI patients.

result, lowered the cost of medicine.

One of the most important advantages of MRI over other diagnostic modalities (such as CT) is the lack of X-ray radiation. This becomes more important in children and young women.

The MRI unit is housed in the aesthetically attractive building that holds a design award from the City of Stockton. In order to operate the magnet, the building had to be shielded from surrounding radio frequencies. Hence during construction, a wire copper mesh was introduced into its construction.

At the present time MRI can be performed on any part of the body. The patients are seen on referral basis only. Going for an appointment requires no special preparation, although patients who are going to have MRI of the abdomen or pelvis are requested not to eat anything for breakfast or lunch. Medication, however, can be continued as usual. At the center the patient is asked to leave all jewelry, keys, credit cards, and any other metallic objects outside the examining room because credit cards will be erased by the powerful magnet, and metallic objects cause image artifacts. Doctors and MRI technologists must know if a patient uses a pacemaker or has an aneurysm clip, cardiac valve, insulin pump, hearing aid, or electrodes. Currently MRI cannot be performed on anybody with a cardiac pacemaker.

Side effects of MRI are not currently known. But doctors prefer not to perform MRI on pregnant women, especially in the first trimester. If imaging of a pregnant woman becomes clinically important, MRI is safer than using X rays.

MRI examinations usually take from 30 to 60 minutes. Radiologists review the results and then discuss the findings with the patient's physician. Currently, Drs. Javad Jamshidi, Dennis Jacobsen, and Chull Song are the primary radiologists at the center.

Researchers point out important and exciting future developments in MRI. Cine cardiac imaging would provide detailed anatomical and functional information about the heart, especially in patients with myocardial infarction and children with congenital heart disease. Vascular imaging or producing pictures of vessels inside the body without the use of X ray and contrast material is another promising research subject. Magnetic resonance spectroscopy is a very complex subject that would provide images of metabolism of sensitive organs such as the brain.

Stockton Cardiology Medical Group Complete Heart Care, Inc.

On a typical day the doctors and staff at Stockton Cardiology Medical Group see an average of 100 patients.

The patients are from all parts of the San Joaquin Valley and the mother lode, many having been referred by their own doctors specifically because of heart problems.

After the patients have been treated, most are usually free to return to their own doctors. However, many continue making regular visits to Stockton Cardiology because they feel more comfortable once under the care of a heart doctor.

Cardiology is the science of taking care of the heart without surgery. The closest a cardiologist will come to surgery is inserting a line through the patient's vein for a pacemaker.

Stockton Cardiology, located in Wood Lane Medical Center at 415 East Harding Way, was founded as a cardiology group in the late 1960s as a partnership and later incorporated as a professional corporation in 1976. The medical staff includes Drs. Edward H. Caul, Leonid G. Kamenetsky, Masanobu Kamigaki, Abbas A. Chothia, Surrender Raina, John A. Bouteller, and George S. Charos. The office staff includes nurse practitioners Yvonne Jackson and Donna Burk along with other nurses, technicians, and technologists. The administrator manages all nonmedical aspects of the business.

The medical office offers a variety of nonsurgical services. In nuclear cardiology, the patient is given an intravenous injection that allows the medical staff to look at the heart through a scanner to determine circulation.

Another procedure, the exercise electrocardiogram test, involves use of a treadmill, bicycle, or a hand ergometer. The latter is a device ideal for those who can not use the treadmill or sit on the bicycle.

Echography, which is an ultrasound test, involves sonar to watch the motion of the heart. Doppler tests are included.

Although there are many kinds of heart problems, one of the more common is angina, a clamping, vice-like feeling in the chest that occurs when the heart is not getting enough circulation. In angina, cholesterol, perhaps, has clogged the arteries in the heart so that it no longer is getting the blood it needs. Any fast movement, exercise, scare, or other stress can bring on chest pains because the heart has started to work extra hard, and its muscles are not getting enough blood. That is when bypass surgery often becomes necessary.

Some people, especially those who lead physically active lives, opt for bypass surgery. However, angina can be controlled with medication if it is taken properly.

Monitored by a doctor and technologist, a patient undergoes a heart test with a Stress Electrocardiogram.

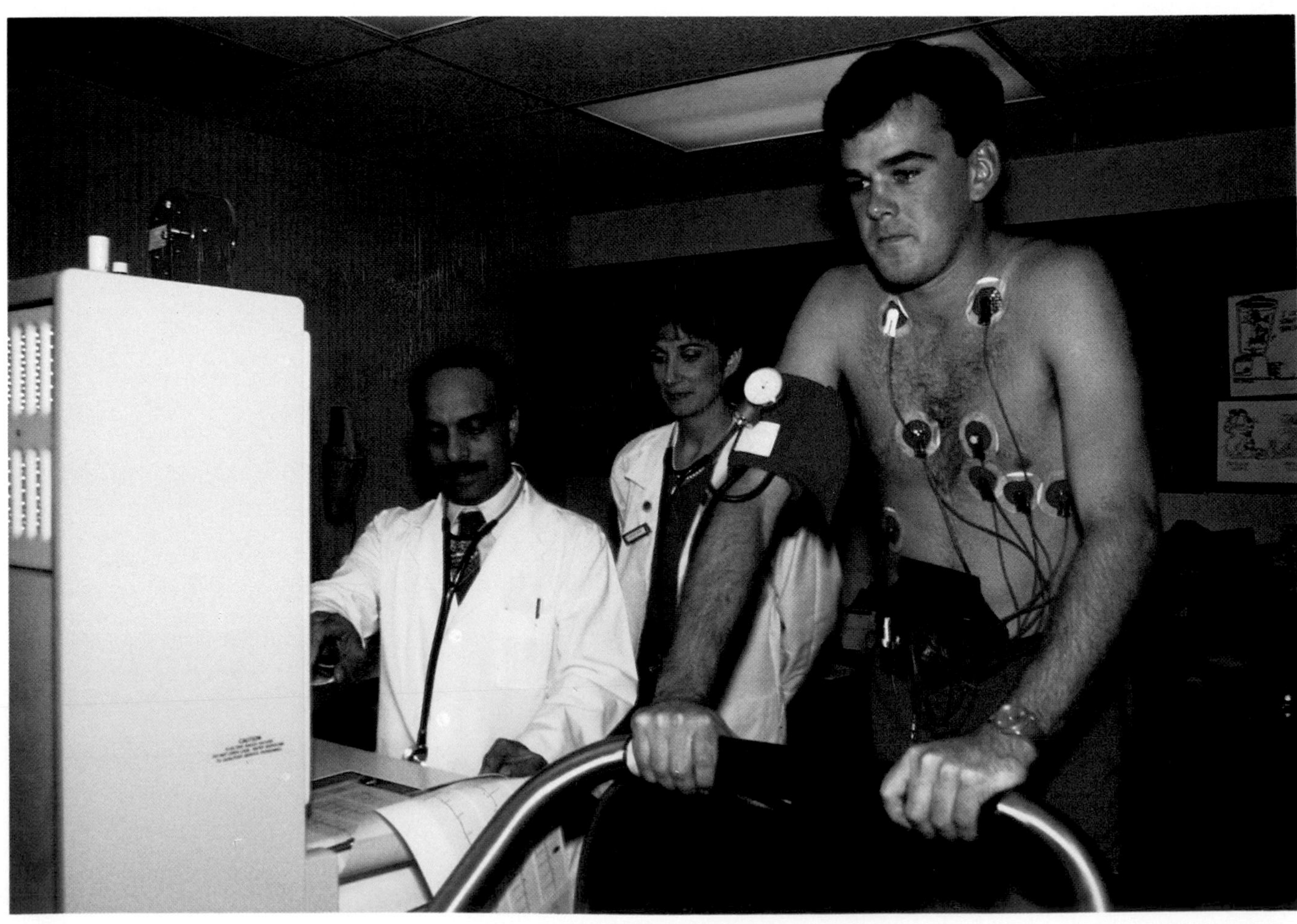

Patrons

The following individuals, companies, and organizations have made a valuable commitment to the quality of this publication. Windsor Publications and the City of Stockton Office of Economic Development gratefully acknowledge their participation in *Stockton: Heart of the Valley*.

American Moulding & Millwork Company*
Beck Development Co., Inc.
Beck Construction Company
Beck and Ratto Realtors, Inc.*
Central State Credit Union*
Chicago Title*
Continental Cablevision*
Corn Products of Stockton*
Daugherty & Company Insurance Brokers, Inc.*
Diehl, Steinheimer, Riggio, Haydel & Mordaunt*
Feldman, Waldman & Kline*
Grant Thornton*
Greater Stockton Chamber of Commerce*
The Grupe Company*
KJOY-AM and KJAX-FM*
McMasters & Westland*
Nestlé Foods Corporation*
Neumiller & Beardslee*
St. Joseph's Medical Center of Stockton*
San Joaquin Magnetic Resonance Imaging Center*
Sharpe Army Depot*
A.G. Spanos Construction, Inc.*
Stockton Cardiology Medical Group Complete Heart Care, Inc.*
Stockton Radiology Medical Group, Inc.*
Teichert Construction*
University of the Pacific*
Valimet Inc.*
Valley Electric Company*

*Participants in Part II, "Stockton's Enterprises." The histories of these companies and organizations appear in chapters 6 through 10, beginning on page 112.

Appendix

STOCKTONIANS OF THE YEAR*

1955 Dean DeCarli
1956 Harvey Stull
1957 Fred Bitterman
1958 George Ernest
1959 J.A. Simpson
1960 Jacob Fetzer
1961 Emerson French
1962 Harold Nelson
1963 Jack O'Keefe
1964 Reed Robbins
1965 Fred Schneider
1966 Michael Canlis
1967 B.L. Faunce
1968 Laurence Drivon
1969 Ort Lofthus
1970 Pearl West
1971 John Cechini
1972 Eugene Castles
1973 D. David Smith
1974 Warren Atherton
1975 Robert Eberhardt
1976 Stuart Gibbons
1977 Pat Noble
1978 Marian Jacobs
1979 Alex G. Spanos
1980 Thelma Stewart
1981 Don Schrader
1982 Helen Crane
1983 'Bing' Wallace
1984 'Fritz' Grupe
1985 Leo C. D'Or
1986 Virgil J. Gianelli
1987 Joseph Serra
1988 Rudy Croce

*Selected by the Stockton Board of Realtors for Community Service and Civic Activities.

Selected Reading

Davis, Olive. *Stockton: Sunrise Port on the San Joaquin.* Northridge, Calif.: Windsor Publications, 1984.

Development Plan for the Stockton Channel. Stockton: Economic Development Administration, 1974.

Dillon, Richard H. *Delta Country.* Novato, Calif.: Presidio Press, 1982.

Gardner, Leonard. *Fat City.* New York: Farrar, Straus and Giroux, 1969. (A novel)

Great Men and Historical Moments in Stockton. Bank of Stockton, 1977.

Hammond, George P. *The Weber Era in Stockton History.* Berkeley, Calif.: The Friends of the Bancroft Library, University of California, 1982.

Hardeman, Nicholas P. *Harbor of the Heartlands.* Stockton: University of the Pacific Holt-Atherton Center for Western Studies, 1986.

Hillman, Raymond W. *Stockton Historical Landmarks.* Stockton: Union Safe Deposit Bank, 1976.

————, and Leonard A. Covello. *Cities and Towns of San Joaquin County, since 1847.* Fresno: Panorama West Books, 1985.

————. *Stockton Through the Decades.* Stockton: Union Safe Deposit Bank and Vanguard Press, 1981.

Kingston, Maxine Hong. *The Woman Warrior.* New York: Knopf, 1976. (A memoir)

Kroll, Cynthia A., and Elizabeth W. Morris. *Economic Conditions and Forces of Change in San Joaquin County.* Berkeley, Calif.: Center for Real Estate and Urban Economics, Institute of Business and Economic Research, October 1988.

Lewis, Cheryl, Toni di Franco, and George H. Lewis. *The Guide to Stockton.* Mercer Island, Wa.: The Writing Works, 1979.

Payne, Walter A., ed. *Benjamin Holt: The Story of the Caterpillar Tractor.* Chapters by Ronald H. Limbaugh, Erling A. Erickson, Roger T. Barnett, Leonard H. Humphreys, and Walter A. Payne. Stockton: University of the Pacific Holt-Atherton Center for Western Studies, 1982.

"San Joaquin County Outlook, '89." Sunday newspaper supplements, G,H,I,J. *The Stockton Record.* January 29, 1989.

Spencer, Horace A. *A Guide to Historical Locations in San Joaquin County.* Stockton: Office of Superintendent of San Joaquin County Schools, 1967.

Stockton, 1988. Greater Stockton Chamber of Commerce and Journal Publications, 1988.

Stockton, Metropolitan Statistical Area (San Joaquin County), 1987-1988. Sacramento: Employment Development Department, 1988.

Thompson, John, and Edward A. Dutra. *The Tule Breakers: The Story of the California Dredge.* Stockton: University of the Pacific, Stockton Corral of Westerners International, 1983.

Thompson, Thomas H., and Albert A. West. *History of San Joaquin County.* Reproduction of 1879 edition. Berkeley, Calif.: Howell-North Books, 1968.

Tinkham, George H. *History of San Joaquin County, California, with Biographical Sketches.* Los Angeles: Historic Records Company, 1968.

Tracy Diamond Jubilee: 1878-1953. Tracy, Calif.: Diamond Jubilee, Inc., 1953.

Welcome to Stockton. Sunday newspaper supplement, *The Stockton Record,* January 31, 1988.

Wik, Reynold M. *Benjamin Holt & Caterpillar: Tracks and Combines.* St. Joseph, Mo.: American Society of Agricultural Engineers, 1984.

Wood, R. Coke, and Leonard A. Covello. *Stockton Memories: A Pictorial History of Stockton, California.* Fresno: Valley Publishers, 1977.

Index